... Better Grammar

Second Edition

Angela Burt

Newmarket Road,
Cambridge CB5 8EG

Newmarket Road,
Cambridge CB5 8EG

Stanle... ...ners) Ltd

Cartoons by Tim Archbold

First published in 1985 (ISBN 0–85950–124–8) by:
Stanley Thornes (Publishers) Ltd
Old Station Drive
Leckhampton
CHELTENHAM GL53 0DN
UK

Second Edition 1991

British Library Cataloguing in Publication Data
Burt, A. M. (Angela M.)
  A guide to better grammar.–2nd. ed.
  I. Title
  428.2

  ISBN 0–7487–0537–6

Typeset by Tech-Set, Gateshead, Tyne & Wear.
Printed and bound in Great Britain at The Bath Press, Avon.

CONTENTS

PREFACE   iv

CHAPTER ONE   **PARTS OF SPEECH**   1
                   Nouns   1
                   Pronouns   7
                   Definite and indefinite articles   18
                   Adjectives   20
                   Verbs   31
                   Adverbs   51
                   Conjunctions   57
                   Prepositions   63
                   Interjections   69

CHAPTER TWO   **SENTENCES**   70
                   Simple sentences   70
                   Compound sentences   72
                   Complex sentences   75
                   Direct and indirect speech   86

CHAPTER THREE   **PARAGRAPHS**   97

ANSWERS TO EXERCISES   111

PREFACE

This new edition of *A Guide to Better Grammar* is the result of an invitation by my publisher to expand the original text (first published in 1985) to bring it into line with the requirements in this area of the National Curriculum. The book now caters very particularly for the needs of pupils at Key Stages 2, 3 and 4, while continuing to be of interest to sixth form and college students and the general public.

The text is now not only much fuller but the presentation is much livelier, thanks to Tim Archbold's cartoons. In addition, I have been permitted to use advertisements, newspaper articles and extracts from handbooks and from contemporary literature to show grammatical points in context rather than having to contrive artificial exercises.

My aim throughout has been to stimulate an interest in our living language and a care in its use. I wanted also to provide the basic terminology for a discussion of language use and its effectiveness, both spoken and written. As Sir John Kingman urges in his 1988 Report of the *Committee of Inquiry into the Teaching of English*:

> If we are able to help pupils function intellectually – and we take this to be a prime purpose of education – we must spend time in English classes examining words and how each contributes to the meaning of a sentence.

Grammatical terminology facilitates such discussion and I have introduced such terms whenever I have felt it to be useful to do so. In the practice exercises I have encouraged analytical discussion and I have structured some for pair and group work.

As in the original guide, students are helped to avoid grammatical errors and confusion in their own writing and they are encouraged to be adventurous syntactically. Misrelated participles, errors in agreement, and vagueness over sentence boundaries are confronted positively, and extended practice is given in converting direct speech to indirect speech (a sophisticated advance in narrative technique), and in combining simple statements in a number of succinct and effective ways. Some students develop these techniques for themselves; I have found that others need structured guidance and encouragement.

In response to many requests, I have added a section on paragraphing. The restructured layout now moves from a consideration of parts of speech, to the analysis of a sentence, and so logically on to the structure of a paragraph.

The book is intended for class use as well as for individual study, and the practice exercises are designed to enable all students to score high marks if they apply carefully the straightforward principles embodied in the text. There is a full explanation of each point, and exercises are set at each stage of an explanation to reinforce understanding. There is a logical progression from one unit to the next within chapters but I have made each unit as self-contained as possible so that a teacher or lecturer can direct a student's attention if he or she is persistently making errors with the construction.

A quarter of a century ago, a disproportionate amount of teaching time was spent on teaching English grammar. Finer points of grammatical dispute and difficulty were relished and many of the exercises seemed especially designed to 'catch out' the unwary student. Few would advocate a return to such practice but the days where one hesitated to use grammatical terms in the classroom are also over. Sir John Kingman and Professor Brian Cox have done much to restore an acceptable balance.

Angela Burt
Exmouth 1990

Chapter One

PARTS OF SPEECH

The words in our language can be divided into different groups according to the work they do. We call these different groups **parts of speech** and each of them has an important function within the sentence.

Nouns

Nouns are 'names of things', as you probably know already, but remember how enormous is the scope of 'things'. As our language has developed, we have given names to all the objects around us (**common nouns**). We have given names to our children, our pets, our villages and towns, our oceans and continents (**proper nouns**); we have given names to our feelings and emotions (**abstract nouns**) and we have special names for collections of things (**collective nouns**) which individually have names already. The more nouns you know the better, because they enable you to express yourself with increased precision.

All the nouns in the passage which follows are underlined.

'But your <u>name</u> is <u>Trimingham</u>, isn't it?' I couldn't help asking. 'You told me it was yourself.' To be on the safe side, and also with a certain <u>guile</u>, I added hastily, 'Mr <u>Trimingham</u>, I mean.'

'You were right the first time,' said he.

Overcome by <u>curiosity</u>, I stared at his odd <u>face</u>, at the <u>scar</u>, the down-weeping blank <u>eye</u>, the upturned <u>mouth</u>, as if they could tell me something. Then I suspected him of teasing me and said:

'But aren't all grown-up <u>men</u> called <u>Mister</u>?'

'Not at all,' he said. '<u>Doctors</u> aren't, for <u>instance</u>, or <u>professors</u>.'

I saw the <u>flaw</u> in this.

But they're called <u>Doctor</u> or <u>Professor</u>,' I said. 'It's a <u>title</u> they have.'

'Well,' he said. 'I have a <u>title</u> too.'

L. P. Hartley The Go-Between (Penguin, 1986)

Practice with nouns

Exercise 1

Look around the room where you are sitting. List all the objects you can see which begin with C.

Exercise 2

Use the letter S this time and supply a proper noun to fit each of these categories.

1) girl's name
2) boy's name
3) a Shakespearian character
4) country
5) day of the week
6) month of the year
7) actress
8) composer
9) town
10) river

Remember that proper nouns begin with a capital letter.

Exercise 3

Matthew has omitted five capital letters in his note to Jake. Can you find five proper nouns without the capital letters they should have?

Dogwood 2528

14 Carlton avenue
Dogwood
21 : 9 : 90

Jake,
　I've managed to get four cheap tickets for the meteor concert at bristol Hippodrome on friday week. Carl and Jerome want two of them and we wondered if you would like the spare one. Give me a ring if you're interested.
　　　　　　　Matthew

P. S. Arms Malone is back on bass and they're doing your favourite song, 'I love you, lorna'.

Abstract nouns

Abstract nouns are names of emotions, qualities, and concepts, such as **joy**, **confidence**, **excellence**.

Exercise 4

Test your vocabulary. Form appropriate abstract nouns from the words in brackets.

1) You could see the _____ on Sean's mother's face when he came in first.　　(proud)

2) I am so touched by your _____ and kindness. (generous)

3) The _____ of the pond should be measured first. (deep)

4) My grandmother rarely mentions the _____ she remembers so clearly in the 1930s.　　(poor)

5) All the other students admired Ali's _____ . He refused to give up.　　(persevere)

Exercise 5

Spell the plurals of these nouns.

ox	turkey	laboratory
fox	soprano	handkerchief
city	princess	mother-in-law
woman	mosquito	

Collective nouns

Collective nouns are names of collections or groups such as a **herd** of cows, a **bouquet** of flowers.

Exercise 6

Give the collective nouns for the following:

1) sheep
2) elephants
3) newly-baked cakes
4) stars
5) taxis
6) lions
7) mackerel
8) poems
9) puppies
10) soldiers

Exercise 7

There are some very beautiful collective nouns such as a wisp of snipe, a charm of goldfinches, an exaltation of larks. You can have fun making up your own. (One of the best I've yet heard is a dampness of babies.) Make up your own collective nouns for:

1) pop-stars
2) schoolboys
3) bicycles
4) flies
5) headmasters
6) nuns
7) dragonflies
8) parents
9) examination results
10) kittens

Remember that when you talk about **a swarm** of bees, you are talking about **one swarm**, and this is **singular**.

A swarm of bees is an impressive sight.

Sometimes, however, it would not make good sense to treat the collective noun as singular. Look at these two examples:

The jury **was** unanimous in **its** verdict.
The jury **were** divided over the issue.

In the first example, the jury is seen as a united group (singular); in the second example the members of the jury are disagreeing with each other and we see them as twelve different people (plural).

'A swarm of bees is singular'

5

Exercise 8

In pairs or small groups, decide whether a singular verb or a plural verb makes better sense in each of the sentences below.

1) A crowd of protesting students (was/were) seen advancing on the British Embassy.
2) Sarah's batch of rock-caves (is/are) completely ruined.
3) The Entertainment Committee (was/were) equally divided over the proposal.
4) The whole gang of football hooligans (has/have) been arrested.
5) The flock of sheep (was/were) effortlessly controlled by the two sheepdogs.
6) A herd of rampaging elephants (is/are) a terrifying spectacle.
7) A huge shoal of fish (has/have) just been spotted off-shore.
8) The jury (was/were) drawn from all walks of life.
9) The jury which was sitting on the hit-and-run case (has/have) been in court for four weeks already.
10) The damaged crate of bananas (was/were) in an appalling state when opened.

Exercise 9

Try your hand at supplying the missing nouns in the following extract. You can check your suggestions against those in the original text by turning to the back of the book.

Nonetheless in the present job _____ , it is very unlikely you will get the first job you try for, so do not narrow down your _____ of employer too much. Applying for a _____ does not commit you to taking the job even if it is offered to you, so apply for as many jobs as take your _____ . You should apply for them all at once. Don't wait for a _____ as a result of an interview before trying for the next job.

It's no help to escape from the _____ of getting a job by 'drifting' into higher _____ . This could just be storing up worse problems later on. It's also a _____ just to leave it all hoping that 'something will turn up', as it probably will not.

Interviews for jobs are much more important than interviews for academic courses. For jobs, you are being judged on very different _____ . After all, interviews are the final part of a selection process covering advertisements, job descriptions and application forms. Careful preparation helps you to make the most of your _____ . If you don't get that one, keep trying for another.

Mary Monro, *Jobs and Careers after A levels* (Hobsons Publishing Co, 1983)

Pronouns

Pronouns take the place of nouns whenever it is convenient within the sentence. They can save a great deal of awkward and tedious repetition.

The pronouns in the extract below are underlined.

'She is waiting. She knows you are here.'
'I do not care if it is the Queen herself. I will not see her.'
'I shall not be present.'
Her cheeks had grown very red, almost as red as

Charles's. For the first – and last – time in his life <u>he</u> was tempted to use physical force on a member of the weaker sex.

But <u>she</u> shook her head.

John Fowles, The French Lieutenant's Woman (Cape, 1969)

These are the most commonly used pronouns:

I know Hong Kong well.	The puzzle baffled **me**.
You are a good friend.	My aunt saw **you**.
He is a kind man.	The whole family like **him**.
She has hurt both legs.	Nobody has met **her**.
It is a pity.	The postman delivered **it**.
We are moving.	British Gas warned **us**.
You must come over.	Your parents advised **you**.
They send their apologies.	The children helped **them**.

I and me

You will see that more than half the pronouns above have two forms. Usually we choose the correct form quite instinctively, but there are a few occasions when we might hesitate. You would probably have no difficulty with these sentences:

Give that to **me**.   (not 'to I')
He did that for **us**.   (not 'for we')
I had lunch with **her**.   (not 'with she')

On the other hand, you might hesitate when two pronouns are used:

√   It is to be shared between **you and me**.
    (not 'you and I')

The pronoun I/me is a difficult one to handle when it is coupled with another pronoun as above or, as it often is, with a noun.

√   She gave the wine to **my husband and me**.
      (not 'to my husband and I')

If ever you find yourself hesitating between I/me in the construction above, always resolve it by simplifying the situation. Deal with the two people separately.

She gave the wine to **my husband**
+
She gave the wine to **me**
= She gave the wine to **my husband and me**.

Consider also these constructions.

My husband and _____ have been invited to supper.
They have invited my husband and _____ to supper.

Once again, temporarily omit the companion and there is no problem.

I have been invited to supper.
My husband and I have been invited to supper.
They have invited **me** to supper.
They have invited **my husband and me** to supper.

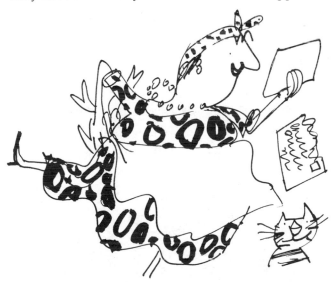

Practice with pronouns

Exercise 10

I or me? Select the correct form of the pronoun to fill the blanks in the sentences below.

1) The rest of the family have planned a surprise for my sister and _____ .

2) The entire staff, including the caretaker and _____ , were questioned by the police.

3) There's really no disagreement between you and _____ .

4) Would you like to come to a disco with my cousin and _____ ?

5) The Museum Director gave permission to my friend and _____ to open the showcase.

6) The pupils gave my colleagues and _____ some beautiful cards and presents.

7) I don't think Brian and _____ will be able to afford it.

8) My year-tutor obviously dislikes my friend and _____ .

9) My brother and _____ shared first prize.

10) Would you do something for my neighbour and _____ ?

Me, myself and I

These forms are sometimes confused. It is incorrect to say:

×   Darren and **myself** are going to Pimlico.

×   My aunt gave Claire and **myself** a present.

Simplify the construction. Once again, deal with the two people separately.

> **Darren** is going to Pimlico.
> **I** am going to Pimlico.
>
> √   **Darren and I** are going to Pimlico.

> My aunt gave **Claire** a present.
> My aunt gave **me** a present.
>
> √   My aunt gave **Claire and me** a present.

The pronoun **myself** is used in very different circumstances. It can be used as an **emphasising pronoun** to add emphasis.

I myself would be the first to admit that I'm lazy.

It can be used as a **reflexive pronoun** to complete the sense of a verb.

I warmed **myself** in front of the fire.
I looked at **myself** in the mirror.

Exercise 11

Look carefully at these ten sentences. In which four of them has **myself** been wrongly used?

1) Matthew and myself will get some bread on the way home.

2) I put it in the drawer myself.

3) I can tell you that it gave both Esam and myself a nasty shock.

4) I shall pamper myself with creams and lotions.

5) As far as my husband and myself are concerned, we never want to see them again.

6) I promised myself a free weekend when we finished the rockery.

7) I saw him myself.

8) I know myself well enough to know my limitations.

9) I pulled myself together and knocked on the door.

10) The first prize was shared by Samuel and myself.

THEIRSELVES and THEMSELFS
do not exist

Note that there is no reflexive or emphasising pronoun spelt

theirselves or **themselfs**

No such form exists. These two errors are mis-pronunciations as well as misspellings.

Consistency and agreement

Consistency in use of 'one'

The pronoun **one** needs care in use. It is important to use it consistently once you start.

> **One** should attempt to keep **one's** garden tidy, whatever the calls upon **one's** time, because **one** doesn't want to annoy **one's** neighbours.

You may feel that **one** is a rather pompous and clumsy pronoun. It is always possible to avoid using it. Use **you** instead.

Each

Each is singular.

> **Each** of them **has** been given a radio. (Don't be distracted by **them**.)

Agreement between nouns and pronouns

Make sure that you match pronouns with the nouns they replace. It is very easy to confuse singular and plural.

X   The effects for the **pupil** concerned will be disastrous, causing **them** endless trouble.

√   The effects for the **pupil** concerned will be disastrous, causing **him** (or **her**) endless trouble.

Exercise 12

Test your understanding of consistency and agreement by making any necessary corrections to these sentences.

1) If one is to look one's best, you must have a daily routine of cleansing and personal care.

2) One never knows when disaster may strike and you should be prepared.

3) A nurse always tries to be as reassuring as possible but they are bound to be honest with you as well.

4) As far as the housewife is concerned, I advise them to return all tins of the affected salmon to the Environmental Health Officer immediately.

5) Each of them are as bad as the other as far as I am concerned.

6) One would hope that something could be done but you can never tell.

7) Each of the holiday chalets are equipped with a refrigerator and a microwave.

8) It is only right that one should help his friends when they are in trouble.

9) A teacher wants to assist their pupils as much as possible but time is very limited.

10) What one experiences during his early years has an effect on you for the rest of your life.

Who and whom

Deciding between the relative pronouns **who** and **whom** can sometimes be difficult. This method may help you.

If you are trying to decide between who/whom in this sentence:

Charles Causley is a poet _____ lives in Cornwall.

Break the sentence into two simple statements:

Charles Causley is a poet.
He lives in Cornwall.

You always use **who** to replace **he** and so now you can make your choice.

Charles Causley is a poet **who** lives in Cornwall.

Similarly, faced with the same choice in this sentence:

Charles Causley is a poet _____ I much admire.

Break the sentence into two simple statements:

Charles Causley is a poet.
I much admire him.

You always use **whom** to replace **him**.

Charles Causley is a poet **whom** I much admire.

Exercise 13

Who or whom?

1) Anna is a girl _____ works very hard.
2) Sadly, we all know _____ has done this.
3) The librarian _____ I consulted was very helpful.
4) The headmaster will know someone _____ can help.
5) Those _____ the gods love they first make mad.
6) Miss Holland, _____ I have known for a number of years, will make an excellent secretary.
7) The person _____ I most admire is my daughter.
8) The young actor _____ I befriended is now famous.
9) The cheat and swindler to _____ you refer will be joining us presently.
10) I don't know _____ is the winner yet.

Who and Whom at the beginning of questions

Who and **whom** at the beginning of questions can also cause difficulty. If you are not sure how your question should begin, try **answering** the question (using the word he or him in your answer).

_____ is there? **He** is there.

You always use **who** to replace **he** and so now you can make your choice.

Who is there?
_____ do you recognise? I recognise him.

You always use **whom** to replace **him** and so now you can make your choice.

Whom do you recognise?

Exercise 14

Who or whom?

1) _____ is there?

2) _____ will you marry?

3) _____ did you see in town?

4) _____ is coming to Sharon's party?

5) _____ cares if the flat is untidy?

6) _____ can we invite to the barbecue?

7) _____ should I believe?

8) _____ will ever understand me?

9) _____ did you pass on the way home?

10) _____ is your brother's blond friend?

Who/whom and that/which

Who/whom are used where we refer to people. **That/which** are used when we refer to things.

He is a man **who** has travelled a great deal.
Anita Brookner is a writer **whom** I admire.

The remark $\left. \begin{array}{c} \textbf{that} \\ \textbf{which} \end{array} \right\}$ really hurt me was that I had big feet.

Sometimes **whom, that**, and **which** are not actually stated but are 'understood' or taken for granted.

Anita Brookner is a writer I admire.
A book I love is *Hotel du Lac*.

Our language is changing slowly all the time as new words are coined and usage changes. Forms and constructions which once seemed clumsy and indeed deplorable can become familiar and acceptable as the decades pass. Notice this process and be alert to changes taking place in your lifetime.

This might be an appropriate opportunity to look back four centuries or so to a translation of the Bible, the Authorised Version, which was published in 1611.

Exercise 15

As an interesting exercise, try to put this extract from the Book of Ruth into good contemporary English and notice all the changes you have to make to spelling, punctuation, vocabulary and grammar. You will find it difficult to match the simplicity and beauty of the Authorised Version but do your best. When you have finished, compare your version with your neighbour's.

> And Ruth said, Intreat me not to leave thee, or to return from following after thee: for whither thou goest, I will go; and where thou lodgest, I will lodge: thy people shall be my people, and thy God my God; where thou diest, will I die, and there will be buried: the Lord do so to me, and more also, if ought but death part thee and me.

Modern English has lost the **thee** and **thou** forms of the pronoun. (The French language, amongst others, has retained it.) **Thee** and **thou** undoubtedly have a warmth and an intimacy which **you** (singular) lacks.

Definite and indefinite articles

All the **definite articles** and **indefinite articles** have been underlined in this extract from a newspaper article.

BRY'S DIY WEDDING!

Herald Exclusive
by Janice Rowe

Bryony Watkins' wedding was full of hitches of the wrong kind – so she is planning to set up a firm to make sure the same doesn't happen to other couples.

But not until she has a re-run of her own wedding and invited all 62 guests back.

Bryony's wedding to taxi driver Michael Watkins last weekend at Tower Street Methodist Church was almost ruined by a catalogue of catastrophes. However, she coped so well with the setbacks she wants to go into the wedding business.

On her big day:

- The cake was not made so Bryony and her friend, Jane Ferris, baked it themselves.
- The wedding car failed to turn up so Grenville Downing of a car sales firm in Exeter drove her to the wedding in his own Jaguar XJ6.
- The flowers failed to appear so Jane and Bryony bought silk flowers and made their own bouquets.
- Only 12 hours before the service the organist phoned in sick so Bryony's uncle had to step in.
- The chief bridesmaid let her down so her daughter came to the rescue.
- And then just when things started to go right at the start of the service the video camera they had hired to record the happy event broke down.

Jane, Bryony and her mum, Elsie Poslett, of Turner Avenue, Exmouth, will now be setting up a wedding business.

The Exmouth Herald, 28 April 1989

Exercise 16

Form small groups and appoint a secretary who will keep a record of your findings and report back to the class at the end.

Compare the extract opposite (noting the use of **the** *definite article* and **a, an, some** *indefinite articles* with the version below where the definite and indefinite articles have been interchanged. The substitutions have been numbered for easy reference.)

1) Which substitutions substantially change the meaning? Choose five examples and explain the effect of the change.
2) Do you find any of the substitutions quite effective?
3) Do any of the substitutions make no sense at all?
4) Why do you think these articles are called definite and indefinite?

BRY'S DIY WEDDING!

Bryony Watkins' wedding was full of hitches of a[1] wrong kind – so she is planning to set up the[2] firm to make sure a[3] same doesn't happen to other couples.

But not until she has had the[4] re-run of her own wedding and invited all 62 guests back.

Bryony's wedding to taxi-driver Michael Watkins last weekend, at Tower Street Methodist Church, was almost ruined by the[5] catalogue of catastrophes.

However, she coped so well with some[6] setbacks she wants to go into a[7] wedding business.

On her big day

● A[8] cake was not made so Bryony and her friend, Jane Ferris, baked it themselves

---

- $\underline{A}^9$ wedding car failed to turn up so Grenville Downing of $\underline{the}^{10}$ car sales firm in Exeter drove her to $\underline{a}^{11}$ wedding in his own Jaguar XJ6.
- $\underline{Some}^{12}$ flowers failed to appear so Jane and Bryony bought silk flowers and made their own bouquets.
- Only 12 hours before $\underline{a}^{13}$ service $\underline{an}^{14}$ organist phoned in sick so Bryony's uncle had to step in.
- $\underline{A}^{15}$ chief bridesmaid let her down so her daughter came to $\underline{a}^{16}$ rescue. And then, when things started to go right, at $\underline{a}^{17}$ start of $\underline{a}^{18}$ service, $\underline{a}^{19}$ video camera they had hired to record $\underline{a}^{20}$ happy event broke down.

Jane, Bryony, and her mum, Elsie Poslett of Turner Avenue, Exmouth, will now be setting up $\underline{the}^{21}$ wedding business.

Adjectives

Adjectives tell us more about nouns and pronouns.

Rory is a **tall**, **thin**, **pale**, **young** man with **straight**, **red** hair and **huge damp** hands.

In the sentence above, it is the adjectives that tell us all the interesting things about Rory. Without the adjectives, this particular statement would not be worth making. Well-chosen adjectives will make your own writing vivid and interesting. Be very selective. Use only those that best convey to the reader what you can see in your mind's eye.

There are nine different kinds of adjectives but all adjectives perform a single function; they tell us more about the nouns and pronouns to which they refer.

In the sentences that follow you will see how the nine different kinds of adjectives (bold type) all tell us more about a noun or pronoun (underlined).

Note It doesn't matter in the least about not knowing the names of the different kinds of adjectives. What does matter is that you should recognise the work each adjective is doing.

<u>She</u> is often **inattentive**.   (adjective of quality)
There were **ten** <u>coins</u> in the purse.   (adjective of quantity)
You're standing on **my** <u>foot.</u>   (possessive adjective)
You're the **very** <u>person</u> I've been looking for.
     (emphasising adjective)
Whose <u>rucksack</u> is this?   (interrogative adjective)
I know <u>someone</u> **whose** <u>father</u> met Lloyd George.
     (relative adjective)
That <u>excuse</u> is simply not good enough.   (demonstrative
     adjective)
What <u>cheek!</u>   (exclamatory adjective)
Mr Poirot telephoned the **Belgian** <u>consul.</u>   (adjective
     formed from proper noun)

In addition, you will find that all four kinds of nouns can be used adjectivally without any change at all to their form.

Tourists enjoy a ride on a **London** <u>bus.</u>   (proper noun
     used as an adjective)
Don't forget your **dinner** <u>money.</u>   (common noun used
     as an adjective)
My boss is always talking about my **attitude** <u>problem.</u>
     (abstract noun used as an adjective)
Here you see the **herd** <u>instinct</u> at work.   (collective
     noun used as an adjective)

Further, you can hyphenate two words and use them adjectivally. Indeed, you can hyphenate as many as are practicable for this purpose.

It's a **dead-end** job.
I find her **couldn't-care-less** attitude infuriating.

Practice with adjectives

Exercise 17

Adjectives, and nouns and hyphenated words used adjectivally have been underlined in this extract from an article in *The Sunday Times*. In pairs, decide to which noun or pronoun each adjective is referring.

The Fillings Bite Back

Neville Hodgkinson investigates the mercury hazard which lurks in our teeth.

Buckingham Palace last week dismissed as 'absolute nonsense' claims that the Princess of Wales has had all the mercury-based amalgam fillings in her teeth removed. According to the reports, she had them replaced with white resin-based composite materials after learning of potentially toxic effects from the old ones.

Nonsense or not, the reports rekindle the worry, especially among those of us with a mouthful of mercury – all black or silver fillings contain it – about whether the metal might be doing us harm. Is there real cause for concern?

---

1) mercury

2) our

3) last

4) absolute

5) all

6) mercury-based

7) amalgam

8) her

9) white

10) resin-based

11) composite   15) black

12) toxic   16) silver

13) old   17) real

14) all

Exercise 18

Write out the 26 letters of the alphabet and use each as the first letter of a vivid adjective. (Use your dictionaries if you must.)

Exercise 19

Ten adjectives have been omitted from this marvellous poem by W. H. Auden which evokes the sights, sounds and movement of the seashore. Read the poem carefully and supply adjectives which you feel would fit sensitively. Then turn to the back of the book to see the words which Auden chose. Compare your choice and his carefully.

Remember that the sound of the words in this poem is just as important as their meaning. You must choose words which not only make good sense but which also sound right.

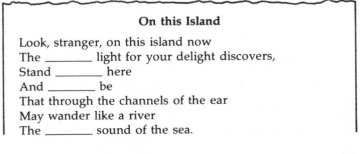

On this Island

Look, stranger, on this island now
The _____ light for your delight discovers,
Stand _____ here
And _____ be
That through the channels of the ear
May wander like a river
The _____ sound of the sea.

Here at the small field's ending pause
When the chalk wall falls to the foam
and its _____ ledges
Oppose the pluck
And knock of the tide,
And the shingle scrambles after the _____ surf,
And the gull lodges
A moment on its _____ side.

Far off like _____ seeds the ships
Diverge on _____ voluntary errands
And its full view
Indeed may enter
And move in memory as now _____ clouds do
That pass the harbour mirror
And all the summer through the water saunter.

W. H. Auden, 'The Island' (*The Penguin Poets*, Faber and Faber, 1958)

Exercise 20

All the proper nouns in brackets have an adjectival form. Use your dictionary to help you if necessary.

1) (Liverpool) traditions
2) (Paris) elegance
3) (Isle of Man) cat
4) (Slav) dances
5) (Norway) ships
6) (Denmark) pastries
7) (Naples) ice-cream
8) (Switzerland) cotton
9) (Dickens) London
10) (George) architecture

Exercise 21

What are the adjectives derived from these nouns?

1) Mountain   mountain_____
2) Circle   circ_____
3) Example   ex_____
4) Parent   parent_____
5) Chaos   chao_____
6) Choir   cho_____
7) Wisdom   wis_____
8) Trouble   trouble_____
9) Giant   gi_____
10) Conscience   conscien_____

Exercise 22

Use these endings to help form adjectives from these verbs.

Each suffix (ending) is to be used *once* only.

–ite, –ic, –some, –ful, –ous, –ant, –ive, –able, –y, –al

1) to sympathise
2) to sleep
3) to quarrel
4) to favour
5) to ridicule
6) to explode
7) to please
8) to criticise
9) to inflame
10) to wake

Position of adjectives

Although in practice adjectives are usually placed directly in front of the noun they are describing (this is rarely the case with adjectives describing pronouns), a great deal of flexibility is possible.

Exercise 23

In pairs, decide how the emphasis is subtly altered as the adjectives take up different positions in these sentences.

1) **Sad** and **lonely**, the woman stood gazing into the lake.
2) The woman stood, **sad** and **lonely**, gazing into the lake.
3) The woman, **sad** and **lonely**, stood gazing into the lake.
4) The woman stood gazing into the lake, **sad** and **lonely**.
5) The **sad**, **lonely** woman stood gazing into the lake.
6) **Sad**, **lonely**, the woman stood gazing into the lake.

Comparison of adjectives

Some adjectives are capable of being used at three levels of comparison:

rich	rich**er**	rich**est**	
silly	sill**ier**	sill**iest**	(Note spelling change)

Longer words form the comparative and superlative differently:

Positive	*Comparative*	*Superlative*
beautiful	**more** beautiful	**most** beautiful
magnificent	**more** magnificent	**most** magnificent
enthusiastic	**more** enthusiastic	**most** enthusiastic

By using **less** and **least** you can go in the opposite direction:

Positive	*Comparative*	*Superlative*
optimistic	**less** optimistic	**least** optimistic
hopeful	**less** hopeful	**least** hopeful

Some words form their comparative and superlative quite irregularly and these forms have to be learnt individually:

Positive	*Comparative*	*Superlative*
bad	worse	worst
good	better	best
many	more	most

Don't mix the two comparative constructions:

| ✓ | fewer | ✗ | more fewer |
| ✓ | more useful | ✗ | more usefuller |

Don't mix the two superlative constructions:

| ✓ | fewest | ✗ | most fewest |
| ✓ | most useful | ✗ | most usefullest |

Don't try to form the comparative and superlative of words which are absolute. **Unique, round, excellent, eternal, perfect,** etc. are as they are. Something is either unique or it is not unique. There are no degrees in between.

Remember the comparative form is used if **two** of a kind are being compared. The superlative form is used if **three or more** of a kind are being compared:

John is the **taller** of the two boys.
Kate is the **youngest** of the five sisters.

Avoid this kind of wild statement using the superlative:

My husband is more handsome than any man I have ever met.

If you read it carefully, you will see why no husband would be pleased by this compliment as it stands. The insertion of **other** restores the husband to his membership of the male sex:

My husband is more handsome than any **other** man I have ever met.

Exercise 24

Some of these sentences need adjustment. Discuss in pairs which ones need to be adjusted.

1) Uncle William is the most generous of my two uncles.

2) I think that the rose is the most loveliest of all summer flowers.

3) Of the two cricket bats, this one is the better.
4) We measured the two rabbit hutches and found the newer one was by far the longest.
5) The first two people to arrive were Parveen and Jane.
6) He is the tallest of his classmates.
7) Sally is the least talented of her sisters.
8) This record is my most favourite.
9) Sina is the most energetic of the pair.
10) *The Housewives' Weekly* has a larger circulation than any magazine in the United Kingdom.

Them and those

Them is a pronoun as we have already seen. Do not make the mistake of using it as an adjective.

✗   Look at **them** flowers.
✓   Look at **those** flowers.

Those is a demonstrative adjective (one which points out). There are four demonstrative adjectives.

What is the point of **this** experiment?
What is the point of **these** experiments?
Pass me **that** spanner.
Pass me **those** spanners.

Whose and who's

These two forms are sometimes confused and yet it is easy to distinguish between them.

Whose (adjective)

The author **whose** first novel was such a success has been found dead.

Whose rugby boots are these?

Who's (contraction of who is or who has)

Who's sitting in my chair?	(= who is)
I know who's going to win.	(= who is)
Who's eaten my Mars bar?	(= who has)
I know who's eaten it.	(= who has)

Exercise 25

Who's or whose?

1) _____ coming tonight?

2) _____ socks are these?

3) Brian has met a man _____ grandmother went down with the *Titanic*.

4) I wonder _____ voice that is.

5) _____ used all my stamps?

6) _____ the winner.

7) _____ car is that?

8) _____ for tennis?

9) Anyone _____ child is under five years of age will be affected.

10) Let me introduce you to someone _____ influenced me more than anyone else I know.

Its and it's

Notice that **its** does not need an apostrophe when it is used as an adjective.

The baby rabbit wrinkled **its** nose.

It needs an apostrophe only when it is a contradiction of **it is** or **it has**.

It's very wet today.   (= it is)
It's been a long wait.   (= it has).

Exercise 26

Its or it's?

1) _____ impossible to judge between them.

2) I know _____ not your fault.

3) Has your chewing gum lost _____ flavour?

4) _____ been a long time since I've won on the Premium Bonds?

5) Just look at that cat washing _____ ears.

6) Your work has lost _____ sparkle.

7) _____ now emerged that he was spying for Russia when he was at the Polytechnic.

8) _____ your birthday. Move to Piccadilly and, if you pass GO, collect £200.

9) Farhana knows the reason why _____ been cancelled.

10) '_____ not fair!' shouted the furious toddler.

Verbs

Of all the ten parts of speech, undoubtedly the most important is the verb. **Without a verb, a sentence is not possible**. Indeed, just one verb can be a sentence in itself, provided that one word is a verb.

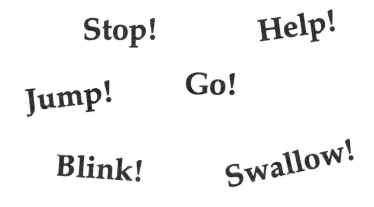

Verbs express actions. (They are 'doing' words.)

The cow **jumped** over the moon.
Aunt Agatha **has swallowed** her last tooth.
Come in, Wendy.
You **will vanish** when I **clap** my hands.
Every time I **pass** George, I **kick** him surreptitiously.
The car **screeched** to a halt, **somersaulted** and **spun** crazily into the ditch.

Verbs also express states. (They can be 'being' words.)

Inspector Jones **is** gravely ill from gunshot wounds.
Your fiancé **seems** very nice.
We **were** all there on time.
The disconnection of your telephone **was** a mistake on our part.
Zoe **became** quite pink at the news.
I **will be** there.

Practice with verbs

Exercise 27

Write out these sentences, underlining each of the twenty verbs. (Each verb is one word only.)

1) We telephoned you immediately.
2) Everyone is very sad at the news.
3) Hurry!
4) The dog seized the lamb and shook it convulsively.
5) I am sorry that I frightened you so.
6) Clint Eastwood spun on his heels and left the saloon.
7) Sean strode across to the window, flung it open, and jumped out.
8) Anna swallowed the oily green medicine and fainted.
9) Blackie miaowed loudly and then purred when she saw the milk.
10) Charles knelt before her, took her left hand in his, and slipped an exquisite sapphire ring on to her third finger.

We can now expand the statement made at the beginning of this unit that every sentence needs a verb.

Every sentence needs a finite verb. A finite verb is a verb that has a subject.

Miranda packed her case.

Miranda = subject, **packed** = finite verb

To find the subject, put **who** or **what** in front of the verb:

Who packed her case? Answer: **Miranda**

Being able to identify subject and verb is not merely an academic exercise; it has a very practical use. Teachers and examiners have complained for years about students who write in the slip-shod 'non-sentences' (without finite verbs) in the belief that they are writing in complete statements. The problem is a grammatical one. It's not simply a matter of when and where to use full stops, for students need to be able to understand the structure of a sentence in order to be able to punctuate it correctly. Sentence structure is dealt with fully in the next chapter of the book but it is useful to be able to identify finite verbs (and their subjects) at this stage.

Exercise 28

All the verbs are in bold type in these sentences. Find their subjects.

1) Mrs Hallan **was** furious because Sandra **laughed** when Karl **fell** off his chair.

2) It **is** very hot, but I **like** it.

3) When Ivy Jenkins **had finished** her weekend shopping, she **treated** herself to a coffee in the Sunlit Cafe.

4) Everybody **knows** how shamefully your husband **has behaved** towards you.

5) Noise **can damage** your health.

Active and passive voice

If the **subject** of the verb is **doing** the action of the verb (as in 'The **dog** bit the man'), the verb is said to be in the **active voice**.

If on the other hand, the **subject** of the verb is **suffering** the action of the verb (as in 'The **man** was bitten by the dog'), the verb is said to be in the **passive voice**.

Exercise 29

Rewrite the sentences in the passive voice.

1) Mr Matthews **has made** the decision.
2) Hailstones **flattened** every lettuce.
3) Hecklers **have interrupted** the Prime Minister repeatedly.
4) The management **will reimburse** all ticket-holders.
5) Viola **makes** the dolls' heads.

6) The French Air Traffic Controllers' strike **delayed** flights by up to 72 hours.
7) I **shall** never **forget** this day.
8) The birds **had eaten** all the nuts.
9) Vandals **will** probably **uproot** every bedding plant and shrub.
10) Everybody here **loathes** cruelty to animals.

Exercise 30

Rewrite the sentences in the active voice.

1) The telephone **was answered** by Lord Kinross.
2) Syllabub **should be eaten** very slowly with a tiny spoon.
3) All his pocket money **has been spent**.
4) The sun **was obscured** by sullen grey clouds.
5) The locks **had been forced** by an intruder.
6) This incident **will** never **be forgotten** by the people of Dominica.
7) Mrs Sinclair **was outraged** at the suggestion.
8) Her answer **was given** in a low voice.
9) When **will** these shirts **be ironed** by Mrs Phelps?
10) The docks strike **has been called** off by the union.

Exercise 31

Which sentence in each pair has its verb in the active voice?

1) a) The dog has bitten the cat again.
   b) The cat has been bitten again by the dog.

2) a) We all enjoyed the Richard Gere film.

   b) The Richard Gere film was enjoyed by us all.

3) a) Smoked mackerel is not liked by everyone.

   b) Not everyone likes smoked mackerel.

4) a) The grass should be cut this weekend.

   b) I should cut the grass this weekend.

5) a) The children cooked supper.

   b) Supper was cooked by the children.

> The meaning of the sentence remains the same (as you have seen) whether the verb is active or passive, but there can be a **subtle change in emphasis and tone** if you change from one to the other. You will be able to judge in context which is best for your purpose.

Non-finite parts of the verb

Finite verbs have subjects; non-finite verbs do not. The non-finite parts of the verb are the infinitive, the participles (past and present) and the gerund.

The infinitive	(... **to enjoy** a pint of beer)
The present participle	(**Speaking** confidentially ...)
The past participle	(**Bewildered** by the noise ...)
The gerund	(... by your **asking** me to be chairman)

The infinitive

The infinitive is usually two words but is sometimes contracted to one.

Emily longed **to go** abroad.
To sit down would be a relief.
Mr Wilberforce asked him **to come**.
I helped her **pack**./I helped her **to pack**.

You may have heard of the grammatical offence of **splitting the infinitive** and have wondered nervously what was involved. Splitting the infinitive simply means separating the two words of an infinitive by putting a word or phrase between them.

Mary claims **to** <u>fully</u> **understand** the problem.
Robert was asked **to** <u>honestly</u> **say** what he felt.

The words underlined in the two examples above are coming between the two words of the infinitive (are splitting the infinitive) and it is usually better to change the word order.

Mary claims **to understand** the problem **fully**.
Robert was asked **to say honestly** what he felt.

There are some occasions when it is better to split the infinitive than to avoid doing so clumsily. As always, you can break the rules most successfully when you know what you are doing.

Exercise 32

Locate the five split infinitives in the following sentences and rewrite.

1) I am writing to most humbly apologise for my inefficiency.
2) Simon tried to pay attention to what was being said.
3) Try to clearly describe what happened.
4) The young man tried to eloquently and persuasively express his deepest feelings.
5) Can I trust you to deliver this?
6) I should like to briefly explain the reasons for this decision.
7) You must try harder.
8) Sophie has decided to leave immediately.
9) It is no good explaining to him what has happened.
10) Do you agree to loyally and unquestioningly observe the rules of the association?

The present participle and the past participle

Participles have two functions. **Participles can help form tenses**.

He was **sleeping**.   (present participle)
He has **slept**.   (past participle)

Participles can be used as verbal adjectives. (Like adjectives they describe nouns and pronouns but like verbs they express actions.)

He stormed out of the room, **slamming** the door loudly as he did so.

The present participle 'slamming' describes the pronoun 'he' as well as telling us what 'he' *did*.

The **survivor, bruised** and **shaken**, staggered to his feet.

The past participles 'bruised' and 'shaken' describe the noun 'survivor' as well as telling us what *has happened* to him.

It is very easy to forget the adjectival force of present and past participles. If you construct a sentence carelessly without making sure that the participle is qualifying the right noun or pronoun, it will simply describe the nearest grammatically likely one.

✕ **Walking** up the garden path, a chipped and blistered **front door** came into view.

This sentence is best corrected by changing the participial construction and making it absolutely clear who is doing the walking (presumably it was *not* the front door).

✓ As I walked up the garden path, a chipped and blistered front door came into view.

Misrelated participles

These are participles which 'relate' to the wrong noun or pronoun.

Exercise 33

Each of these sentences contains a misrelated participle. Rewrite them so that they read more naturally.

1) Stumbling along the road in the dark, a sports car knocked her down.
2) Examining the diamond very carefully, it became clear to the dealer that it was a very special one indeed.
3) Driving into the village, the church will be on your left.
4) Having climbed the hill, their energy was well rewarded by the splendid view.
5) Being a naturally honest person, your accusation hurt me very much.
6) Walking along the road, the lilac and the laburnum looked beautiful.
7) Sitting in the deckchair, a wasp stung him.
8) While imprisoned at Strangeways, the chaplain came to see him.
9) Roasted carefully, the whole family enjoys pork.
10) While travelling to Adelaide, disaster struck.

The gerund

Another name for the gerund is **verbal noun** and this describes its function very clearly. Gerunds combine the *naming* power of a noun with the *doing* power of a verb.

Weeping will achieve nothing.
Your **apologising** so promptly has certainly helped.

In the gerunds above, the sense of *doing* is very strong.

As gerunds are verbal nouns, they need adjectives to describe them.

√ **Your apologising** so promptly has certainly helped.

× **You apologising** so promptly has certainly helped.

Exercise 34

Correct the underlined errors.

1) Do you mind <u>me</u> sitting here?

2) No one will object to <u>him</u> joining the group.

3) As a result of <u>us</u> complaining to the examination board, the syllabus was amended.

4) Excuse <u>me</u> asking but I think you need help.

5) Would you agree with <u>us</u> buying the house next door?

Exercise 35

This is a revision exercise. All the finite and non-finite verbs have been printed in bold type in the passage below. Read the passage and then answer the questions which follow.

WE **HAVE** BRANCHES ALL OVER

It **is** Tuesday and I **am standing** next to Neil Kinnock. From time to time, I **nod** deferentially towards him; occasionally, indeed, I **bow** quite low in his direction – some **might say** I **scrape** – and every time this **happens**, David Owen (**rooted** to a spot a few yards off) **trembles** violently.

For here, in the sunny quadrangle of Higham Lane School, the Leader of the Opposition **is** an ornamental cherry and I **am** a whitebeam. What David Owen is though **remains**, as ever, anybody's guess, since, as ever, his label is **obscured**.

We **are**, in short, trees. **To be** yet more punctilious, we **are** in short trees. Others of our peers **are** soon **to be enrooted**: Germaine Greer **is coming**, and Bryan Gould, and Margaret Drabble and Rachael Heyhoe Flint. What **are** we all doing here?

We **are** all, in this case, **being** 50 years old. That **is** because Higham Lane School **is** 50 years old and its **enterprising** head, Alan Breed, **has come** up with the **engaging** wheeze of **commemorating** the milestone by **inviting** 50 quinquagenarians **to dig** a hole and to **'plant'** themselves.

Alan Coren, *The Times*, 23 June 1989 (adapted)

1) What is the subject of **have** in the title?

2) List the eight finite verbs to be found in the first paragraph.

3) Find a past participle in the first paragraph that is used adjectivally.

4) Find a past participle in the second paragraph that is used to help form a tense.

5) Which finite verb in the second paragraph is in the passive voice?

6) Infinitives can be active or passive. Find an example of each in the third paragraph.

7) What are the two functions a present participle can perform? Find an example of each in the last paragraph.

8) Find the two gerunds in the final paragraph.

Exercise 36

All the words in the list below can be used as verbs and can be used as nouns (although pronounced with the stress on the other syllable in some cases). Compose two sentences for each word, using it first as a noun and then as a verb. (Make adaptations, if you wish, to the form when you use it as a verb.)

1) incline
2) fire
3) refuse
4) prize
5) resort
6) spell
7) permit

8) entrance
9) temper
10) clutch
11) grate
12) hamper
13) cough
14) project

15) stem
16) incense
17) sense
18) form
19) pine
20) ferret

Tenses and their use

All finite verbs have tenses. Tenses show **when** the action of the verb takes place.

> **Today** he **sleeps**
> **Yesterday** he **slept**
> **Tomorrow** he **will sleep**

These are the simple forms of these tenses. There are others which introduce new subtleties. Tenses not only make it clear when an action occurs but they can also indicate the duration of an action and whether it is yet completed.

There are various forms of tenses in **four** time zones: **present, past, future**, and **future in the past**. Some of them, as you can see, are really quite complicated constructions.

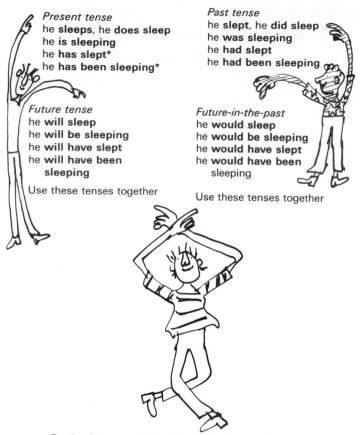

Present tense
he **sleeps**, he **does sleep**
he **is sleeping**
he **has slept***
he **has been sleeping***

Future tense
he **will sleep**
he **will be sleeping**
he **will have slept**
he **will have been
sleeping**

Use these tenses together

Past tense
he **slept**, he **did sleep**
he **was sleeping**
he **had slept**
he **had been sleeping**

Future-in-the-past
he **would sleep**
he **would be sleeping**
he **would have slept**
he **would have been**
sleeping

Use these tenses together

Don't mix tenses in the left-hand column with tenses
in the right-hand column

*Two of the forms of the present tense may cause momentary
difficulty. **He has slept** and **he has been sleeping** sound like
forms of the past tense but they are correctly listed with
present tense. The listing makes sense because they are forms
which **bring the action up to the present moment**.

He **has slept** all day but **now** he is awake.
Today we **have painted** the sitting-room.

Sequence of tenses

Use tenses from the left-hand column together or tenses from the right-hand column. Present and future tenses go together, and past and future-in-the-past go together too. Usually we get the sequences of tenses right instinctively but it's useful to know that there is a 'rule-of-thumb' to help you if ever you are in doubt.

He **says**	that he **is asking** his boss for a rise.
	that he **has asked** his boss for a rise.
	that he **will ask** his boss for a rise.
He **said**	that he **was asking** his boss for a rise.
	that he **had asked** his boss for a rise.
	that he **would ask** his boss for a rise.
✗	He **said** that he **will ask** his boss for a rise.
✓	He **said** that he **would ask** his boss for a rise.

Exercise 37

Practise your understanding of the sequence of tenses by correcting the form of the tense printed in bold type below.

1) I should be so grateful if you **will reply** by return of post.

2) I heard last week that he **has crashed** his car.

3) The suspect went to France so that he **can escape** arrest.

4) Mrs Brown agreed that it **will be** a great improvement.

5) My father promised that he **will come** to us next Christmas.

Tricky past tenses

Some verbs can behave unpredictably. A small child, learning to talk, often makes mistakes which are amusing to adults and to older brothers and sisters.

I goed out (for **I went out**)
I swimmed (for **I swam**)

The mistakes are really quite sensible ones, as you will see if you examine them. The child has grasped the pattern of most past tenses.

I carry   I carri**ed**/I have carri**ed**
I hope   I hope**d**/I have hope**d**

Unfortunately, *go* and *swim* do not follow this pattern and have to be learnt the hard way.

I go   **I went/I have gone**
I swim   **I swam/I have swum**

If you are uncertain of the past tense of a verb, remember that your dictionary will help you. If the verb has irregular parts, they will be listed.

Exercise 38

Try to complete these past tenses correctly.

1) Clare has _____ all her presents.   (choose)

2) However, she hasn't _____ them yet.   (buy)

3) We _____ Mr and Mrs Al-Sharae years ago.   (know)

4) The Post Office has _____ a lot of business this year. (lose)

5) The suspicious-looking man _____ my house four times this morning.   (pass)

6) The nurse _____ the collar of his shirt.   (loosen)

7) The pattern was intricately _____ .   (weave)

8) Both children were sure they had _____ Father Christmas.   (hear)

9) Our horses were _____ in the next village.   (shoe)

10) Some very interesting items were _____ to the museum for identification.   (bring)

11) Nobody _____ the second course.   (eat)

12) Mrs Hussain burst into tears and was gently _____ out of the room.   (lead)

13) I _____ you with my own eyes.   (see)

14) We should like to thank all parents for the time which they have _____ so generously.   (give)

15) Mr Talal _____ us last year.   (teach)

16) Charles _____ Tom a pound very reluctantly.   (lend)

17) The two little boys _____ in a cupboard under the stairs.   (hide)

18) I _____ my homework last night.   (do)

19) Nick _____ the biggest cake, as usual.   (choose)

20) The police _____ him as soon as he came down.   (catch)

Shall/will

Future

If you want simply to indicate future time, the inevitability of certain events occurring in the simple march of time, use this pattern:

I	**shall** sleep	we	**shall** sleep
you(s)	**will** sleep	you(pl)	**will** sleep
he/she/it	**will** sleep	they	**will** sleep

Determination against all odds

If you reverse **shall** and **will**, you introduce a new element:

> I **will** come to the party. (that is – **nothing will stop me!**)
> You **shall** apologise. (that is – **if I have anything to do with it!**)

A very useful pair of sentences to remember in this connection:

> I **shall** be drowned and no one **will** save me.
> I **will** be drowned and no one **shall** save me.

The first sentence indicates the despair of someone who can foretell the future and doesn't like the prospect one little bit.

The second sentence indicates a determination to commit suicide by drowning at all costs.

Exercise 39

Shall or will?

1) I _____ come and see you tomorrow, if all goes well.

2) _____ you have time to iron my blouse?

3) I promise them I _____ do my very best to get the decision reversed.

4) You _____ listen to me! I _____ use force if necessary.

5) We _____ expect you on the last train, as you say.

Should/would

I	**should** know	we	**should** know
You(s)	**would** know	you(pl)	**would** know
he, she, it	**would** know	they	**would** know

I should be grateful if **you would** send a receipted invoice.

Exercise 40

Reversing should/would also changes the meaning subtly.
Show your understanding of this by completing the sentences
below.

1) I would diet _____

2) I should like _____

3) He should pay you rent _____

4) He would pay you rent _____

5) It should be Jane's turn to arrange the flowers _____

Agreement between verbs and nouns

Take care to match plural nouns with plural verbs, and singular
nouns with singular verbs. This advice may sound obvious
but it can sometimes be difficult to recognise which noun
should control the verb in this way.

√   The **variety** of biscuits, cakes and sandwiches <u>was</u>
enormous.

Three plural nouns come between the noun and the verb than
goes with it but these should not distract us from the basic
structure of the sentence. It is the **variety** that is **enormous** not
the biscuits, cakes and sandwiches.

Exercise 41

Supply the correct form of the verb in these sentences. Take
great care to match singular subjects with singular verbs,
and plural subjects with plural verbs.

1) Both cats _____ chasing butterflies.   (enjoy/enjoys)

2) A swarm of bees _____ supposed to be lucky.
   (is/are)

3) All but my Uncle Laurie _____ been invited.
(has/have)

4) The choice of academic and recreational courses _____ quite exciting.   (is/are)

5) Each candidate _____ received the results by post this morning.   (has/have)

COULD OF/WOULD OF/SHOULD OF/ MIGHT OF
do not exist

There is no such form as could of, would of, should of, and might of. The mistake arises from trying to write down the **sound** of the contraction **could've, would've, should've, might've.**

Although these contractions are rarely written, we do **say**:

I **would've** liked to help you.
You **should've** phoned me.
He **could've** told me to my face.
Ben **might've** passed the examination.

These contractions are used quite freely in conversation. In speech they sound natural enough but written down they look rather odd. Therefore, when you write, it is probably better to write **have** in full rather than **'ve**. In formal writing, contractions and abbreviations are usually inappropriate anyway.

I **would have** liked to help you.
You **should have** telephoned me.
He **could have** told me to my face.
Ben **might have** passed the examination.

Adverbs

Adverbs tell us more about verbs and, by telling us **where** something happened, **how** something was done, **when** so-and-so was pelted with eggs, supply much of the precise detail we need if we are to visualise the incident that is being described. In addition, adverbs like **extremely, scarcely, exceedingly, nearly, very** (used with adjectives and other adverbs) increase this precision of description.

He looked at me **contemptuously**.
I **instantly** offered to resign.
The stall-holder smiled **rather uneasily**.
I stood **here** while the murder took place.

Practice with adverbs

Exercise 42

Ten adverbs have been omitted from this extract from *Roses of Eyam*. Try your hand at supplying vivid and appropriate ones. (Don Taylor's adverbs are given at the back of the book.)

People come out of their houses only when they have to, and move _____ and hooded about their business. Some _____ look out, and scurry to the well and back for water; others carry or wheel their dead towards the fields. Single figures walk _____ and alone along the street, deep in their private despair. We see, if possible inside and outside the houses, the slow ordeal of waiting and the death. Music may be used, to accentuate the stylisation of the scene.
  Marshall Howe enters alone.

Howe   So _____ the gates are closed and the ordeal
        begins. Grass grows in the empty streets. You can

_____ see it growing, as the sun pours down on our sweating, infested cottages. Shut in on our own families, _____ going out, seeing no one, man, woman and child, each one faces his terror. We shutter our hearts, and lock _____ hope, and die as _____ we can, as the hot days intensify the slaughter. The last coffins were made in June, when the bodies multiplied _____ than one man's hands could work, and in July those hands too were stilled.

Don Taylor, *Roses of Eyam* (Samuel French, 1976)

Exercise 43

Complete these sentences with vivid adverbs. Do not use any adverb more than once in the course of the exercise.

1) The cat stretched _____ .

2) The boy drank _____ .

3) The girl laughed _____ .

4) The teacher smiled _____ .

5) The wind blew _____ .

6) The old man walked _____ .

7) The rhythm beat _____ .

8) The clock ticked _____ .

9) The woman spoke _____ .

10) The child poked out his tongue _____ .

Comparison of adverbs

Adverbs can be compared in the same way as adjectives.

Monosyllabic adverbs usually form the comparative by adding –**er** and the superlative by adding –**est**:

Positive	Comparative	Superlative
hard	harder	hardest
long	longer	longest
near	nearer	nearest

Most other adverbs follow the more/most pattern:

Positive	Comparative	Superlative
slowly	**more** slowly	**most** slowly
greedily	**more** greedily	**most** greedily
proudly	**more** proudly	**most** proudly

Some adverbs are irregular:

Positive	Comparative	Superlative
well	**better**	**best**
badly	**worse**	**worst**
much	**more**	**most**
little	**less**	**least**

Exercise 44

Correct the errors in these sentences.

1) Jim runs much quicker than Jeremy.

2) Of the two children, Claire works best.

3) You've done it wrong.

4) I'm afraid you sang even worser than I did.

5) Could you deliver the milk more early in future?

6) Ray writes the neatest of all of us.

7) The slowlier you go, the better it will be.

8) Parveen cleaned the blackboard as careful as she could.

9) I thought that Susan danced more graceful than anyone else.

10) Steve did the task thoroughly and he did it good.

Double negatives

Be careful not to use two negative words in one sentence which will cancel each other out. 'Charles did **not** eat **no** apples' means that he was eating apples!

If you want to have Charles abstaining from apples, you have a choice of constructions. Use either **not** or **no** separately but don't use them together.

Charles ate **no** apples.
Charles did **not** eat any apples.

Watch **hardly** very carefully. It too has a negative force. 'Charles did **not** eat **hardly** any apples' means he ate quite a few but it's rather clumsy expressing it this way!

Owing to and due to

The distinction between **owing to** and **due to** is becoming blurred in modern usage. However, it is one that you may care to observe.

Owing to

This has the force of an adverb and refers to a verb.

Owing to your laziness, we **lost** the order.
The match **was cancelled, owing to** the snow.

Due to

This has the force of an adjective and refers to a noun or pronoun.

The **loss** of the order, **due to** your laziness, has been discussed by the Board of Directors.
The **cancellation, due** to snow was not unexpected.

Exercise 45

Use **owing to** or **due to** as traditional correctness would demand.

1) The lower block was evacuated _____ a bomb scare.

2) _____ popular demand, *The Sound of Music* will be shown next Christmas on BBC2.

3) _____ unforeseen circumstances, the auditions will be held a week later.

4) The verdict was death _____ drowning.

5) The increase in sales _____ better advertising was short-lived.

Position of 'only'

The adverb **only** is often used very carelessly by those who do not realise that its position has a vital effect on meaning.

Only Bernard wears green shoes.
                                    (Nobody but Bernard . . .).
Bernard **only** wears green shoes.
                                    (He does nothing else to them . . .).
Bernard wears **only** green shoes.   (No other colour . . .).
Bernard wears green shoes **only**.
                            (No other colour . . . /no other clothes).

Care in the position of only is clearly needed. The rule is straightforward. You place **only** next to the word you want it to modify. It is usually best to place it in front but sometimes it can follow.

Exercise 46

Explain the difference in meaning in the following:

1) a) Only children enjoy ice-cream in the summer.
   b) Children enjoy only ice-cream in the summer.
   c) Children enjoy ice-cream only in the summer.

2) a) Only fish and chips are sold here on Wednesdays.
   b) Fish and chips are only sold here on Wednesdays.
   c) Fish and chips are sold here only on Wednesdays.
   d) Fish and chips are sold only here on Wednesdays.

3) a) Only coffee will be served at 10 a.m.
   b) Coffee will be served only at 10 a.m.
   c) Coffee will only be served at 10 a.m.

Conjunctions

Conjunctions join

There are two kinds of conjunctions, **co-ordinating** and **subordinating**.

Co-ordinating conjunctions

The most common co-ordinating conjunctions are **and, but, or**. These are very familiar words but you do need to select the one you need very carefully. It is surprising how often an inappropriate choice is made.

Co-ordinating conjunctions can join single words:

fish **and** chips
tired **but** happy
gin **or** whisky

They can join phrases:

detested by men **but** adored by women

They can join **sentences** by replacing full stops, question marks and exclamation marks:

He knocked at the door. He didn't come in.
He knocked at the door **but** he didn't come in.

Will you take the car? Will you go by train?
Will you take the car **or** will you go by train?

Drop your gun! Put your hands up!
Drop your gun **and** put your hands up!

Subordinating conjunctions

Subordinating conjunctions also join but they use a different process.
Co-ordinating conjunctions join two **equals** and they remain **equals**.

Subordinating conjunctions join statements by making one **less important** than the other. One statement becomes the **main** statement and the other a **subordinate** supporting one.

Naomi was very clever. She failed the entrance exam.
Although Naomi was very clever, she failed the entrance exam.

The is an effective way of joining because the subordinating conjunction helps to emphasise the connection in sense between the two sentences.

Practice with conjunctions

Exercise 47

Use **and**, **but**, **or**, as appropriate.

1) I think I have passed GCSE English this time _____ I am not sure.

2) I can't decide whether to go to the theatre _____ the cinema tonight.

3) Mr Denzi likes the lad _____ he knows he's incurably lazy.

4) Lola has become depressed _____ listless.

5) Your money _____ your life!

6) The young mother listened carefully to the Health Visitor's advice _____ felt reassured.

7) Simon did what he was told _____ he was seething inwardly.

8) Will you answer the phone _____ shall I?

9) Uncle Fred enjoyed the evening very much _____ said so.

10) Mudstained _____ exhausted, they trudged home.

Exercise 48

Complete these sentences.

1) I can't remember in which book I saw the reference to Tennyson's handwriting but . . .

2) The Board of Directors will remain unchanged and . . .

3) You will either come home at a reasonable time or . . .

4) Sean Connery was offered the chance of playing James Bond again but . . .

5) The toddler had become separated from her frantic mother and . . .

6) Twenty years passed before the lovers met again but . . .

7) Francis strode across to the window, flung it open and . . .

8) You must leave the country or . . .

9) We telephoned you immediately but . . .

10) Juliet swallowed the potion and . . .

Exercise 49

Select an appropriate conjunction from those given below to complete these ten sentences.

unless because whenever if that so that while as if before where as although since

1) _____ the snow was deep, Alison was determined to get to school.

2) _____ you are sure, I should love to have it.

3) _____ it is the firm's policy to encourage initiative, we are promoting you.

4) I know _____ we are early.

5) _____ there is a thunderstorm, our cat hides under the bed.

6) Your mother looks _____ she's very angry.

7) I think I had better explain the rules _____ there is no misunderstanding.

8) _____ we hear from you before Friday, we shall assume you are not coming.

9) _____ you wish, I'll write to him.

10) _____ Paul went to bed, he put the cat out.

Exercise 50

Using any conjunctions you wish, join the following pairs of sentences.

1) You want to fight decay. Clean your teeth after every meal.

2) I know you took the money. I saw you go to his locker.

3) Shaun is very immature. I can't help liking him.

4) You left the house. Marva phoned.

5) Anna had accepted the post. She began to have doubts. She had no experience of bookkeeping.

6) You are no better in the morning. Call me.

7) I asked her thirty years ago to be my wife. She has finally agreed to marry me.

8) I cannot come. I have nothing to wear.

9) You are small. You are strong.

10) Your brother enjoys orienteering. He should join us.

Exercise 51

The conjunctions have been omitted from the following extract. Complete the extract using appropriate conjunctions.

Beware of cyclists

_____ cyclists are a nuisance _____ not depends mainly upon _____ you live _____ the time of day. Either way, beware. _____ you don't give cyclists sufficient room _____ you pass them, you could easily fail yourself. Often they wobble precariously, so take this into account. _____ a cyclist starts to move out into the road _____ you are approaching a junction, slow down to anticipate his next move.

Animals in the Road

Apart from dogs straying on to the road, the most likely animal you'll meet is the horse. Horses are usually nervous. So give them a wide berth _____ you pass, slowing down _____ keeping engine revs to a minimum.

On country lanes, you may meet flocks of sheep, _____ herds of cattle being driven to pasture. _____ you get caught behind them, don't get impatient. Just trail behind very slowly, _____ don't try to overtake. _____ they're approaching you, stop _____ allow them to pass. The examiner would expect you to pass in a sensible _____ controlled manner, _____ under no circumstances to sound your horn.

Derek Fairman, *Pass First Time: The Learner's Guide to the Driving Test* (Macdonald Orbis, 1985)

NOT ONLY ... BUT ALSO

It's well worth taking care with the positioning of the two parts of this construction. Used carelessly, the effect is jumbled and clumsy.

X   Joan not only was very pretty but was also very clever.

√   Joan was **not only** very pretty **but also** very clever.

Used carefully, the sentence has a pleasing balance with the emphasis just where it should be.

Exercise 52

Using the construction **not only ... but also**, join these statements. (Modify the wording if you wish.)

1) Clare is a good swimmer. She is an excellent flautist.

2) Marcel is interested in vintage cars. He is interested in old agricultural machinery.

3) The girls beat the boys at hockey. They beat them at basket-ball.

4) He stole the money. He told me a lie.

5) She was hurt. She was bewildered.

EITHER . . . OR/NEITHER . . . NOR

Don't mix these two constructions.
Neither . . . or is wrong.

Jake is **either** brave **or** very foolish.
Jake is **neither** young **nor** pretty.

Exercise 53

Complete correctly.

1) I refuse either to confirm _____ to deny the matter.

2) The essay was neither well written _____ relevant.

3) You are being neither fair _____ open about this matter.

4) Either she leaves _____ I do.

5) Neither Louise _____ her brother likes vegetables very
   much.

Prepositions

It is very difficult to define prepositions in any clear and
helpful way. It would be better to look at some examples:

The cat sat **on** the mat.
You cannot leave **without** permission.
My parents stayed in the hotel **near** Lake Banyo.
What have you heard **about** him?
Zoe and Tommy shared the sweets **between** them.
The scarf was a present **from** Justin.

You will see that the prepositions (**bold type**) are usually very small words. They are used with nouns and pronouns (underlined) and they serve to show the connection between the noun or pronoun they govern and the rest of the sentence.

Remember that they are used with nouns and pronouns, and you are less likely to confuse them with adverbs. Some words can be used as both prepositions *and* adverbs. A few of these are illustrated below. Note how the prepositions refer always to a noun or a pronoun; the adverbs never do.

Prepositions	Adverbs
Jump **on** the bus.	Jump **on**
Talk **about** the weather.	Run **about**
Join **in** the discussion.	Join **in**

Ending a sentence with a preposition

Should one ever end a sentence with a preposition? Popular folklore has it that it should *never* be done but this is not so. Indeed there are some occasions when to avoid using a preposition would be both clumsy and pompous:

✗　**For** what is this?　(Clumsy and pompous!)
✓　What is this **for**?

On the other hand, if the use of a preposition at the end of a sentence *can* be conveniently avoided, then do so:

✗　He was a man whom it was hard to sympathise **with**.　(Ugly!)
✓　He was a man **with** whom it was hard to sympathise.

You need to have considerable foresight to use a preposition in this way mid-sentence. In speech, it is very difficult indeed to anticipate to this extent and we are frequently less formal. In the following pair of examples, while we should write the second, we should probably say the first:

✓　This is something I have always objected **to**.
✓✓　This is something **to** which I have always objected.

Often prepositions are used quite unnecessarily:

✗ Where are you going **to**?

✓ Where are you going?

✗ You should not use a preposition to end a sentence **with**.

✓ You should not use a preposition to end a sentence.

Don't skimp on prepositions. Be very careful not to skimp on prepositions when using two constructions which need a different preposition for each. Don't try to economise by making one preposition do the work for both:

✗ Ian was resentful and hostile **to** all in authority.

✓ Ian was resentful **of**, and hostile **to**, all in authority.

Even better reconstruct the sentence:

✓✓ Ian was resentful **of** all authority and hostile **to** it.

Practice with prepositions

Exercise 54

Supply the missing prepositions.

1) I prefer sprouts __to__ cabbage.

2) The committee reluctantly agreed __to__ the request for more payphones.

3) Mr Norman was a teacher who inspired me __with__ a love of poetry.

4) Roger Neill is an authority __on__ Dartmoor letterboxes.

5) Arnold Bennett died __of__ typhoid fever.

6) Don't meddle __in__ matters you don't understand.

7) I was furious _with_ the carpet fitters who never came when I expected them.

8) We differ _from_ you in that respect.

9) Have you noticed how proud she is _of_ her new car?

10) Most pupils would object very strongly _to_ being fined for unpunctuality.

Exercise 55

Correct the ten errors made in the use of prepositions.

1) The new recruit was angered and disgusted by the NCO's attitude.

2) Where is my pencil to?

3) To whom are you writing the letter to?

4) My father persisted on giving everyone another sherry.

5) Compare this diamond against that and see the difference.

6) The faulty goods were returned back to the firm.

7) The apparatus comprised of a bunsen burner, a large beaker and some glass tubing.

8) The ransom payment was shared between Scarface, Shorty and Joe the Fingers.

9) Her haughtiness is something up with which I am not prepared to put.

10) I twisted my ankle when I jumped off of the bus.

Exercise 56

This exercise is difficult but do use a dictionary if you are uncertain. Use each of these verbs in a sentence with an appropriate preposition.

1) dissuade
2) gloat
3) aspire
4) encroach
5) comply

6) centre
7) advance
8) protest
9) consist
10) revolve

Exercise 57

Use each of these adjectives in a separate sentence with the preposition that usually goes with it.

1) sympathetic
2) indifferent
3) deficient
4) similar
5) capable

6) different
7) oblivious
8) responsible
9) ignorant
10) superior

LIKE and AS

Take care with **like** and **as**. They have a distinct job to do and they sound ugly if they are confused.

Like is a preposition linking nouns and pronouns to the rest of the sentence.

Take a girl **like** you.
You look **like** your mother.
Like most small boys, Shaun hated having his hair washed.

As is a subordinating conjunction:

As you are so busy, I won't come in.
You look **as** if you have seen a ghost.
It happened exactly **as** Jason has described it.

Exercise 58

Like or **as**?

1) Dino whistles just _as_ his father used to.

2) You are just _like_ him.

3) Barry fought _like_ a little tiger.

4) It is just _as_ I expected.

5) My small son threw his shoebag in the corner just _as_ he always does.

6) _Like_ you, he enjoys astronomy.

7) I cannot trust people _as_ you do.

8) _Like_ most of us, he sometimes loses his temper.

9) You'll find a bargain _as_ you always do.

10) Adelaida will have her own way _as_ you would expect.

Interjections

Interjections are exclamations or asides which are inserted into a sentence but always remain grammatically quite separate:

Hooray, we break up tomorrow!
Hooray! We break up tomorrow.
You will, **however**, be expected to work very hard throughout the summer.

The most common exclamatory interjections are:

Oh! Ah! Ooh! Wow! Ugh! Phew! Sh! Hurrah! Hooray! Hush! Bravo! Hear, hear! Ha, ha!

Here are some archaic ones which you may meet in your reading:

Zounds! Marry! Pardee! Hark! Lo! Pshaw! Ho! Bah! Begad! Alack! Hist! Huzza! Fie! Heigh-ho! Alas!

Exercise 59

Imagine you are writing an historical novel. Compose sentences of dialogue (using archaic interjections) to express the following emotions.

1) anger   3) regret   5) alarm
2) amusement   4) contempt

Exercise 60

Compose sentences containing interjections to be used in a modern novel to express these emotions.

1) delight   3) grief   5) reproof
2) astonishment   4) approval

Chapter Two

SENTENCES

There are three kinds of sentences: command, question and statement.

Command Catch that man!
Question Is your confidence at a low ebb?
Statement The drug pusher was arrested while drinking in The Slug and Lettuce.

Commands, questions and statements can be structured as simple or compound or complex sentences. The examples given above were all of simple sentence and this is where we shall begin in our examination of the structure of sentences.

Simple sentences

A simple sentence has just one finite verb. A finite verb is a verb that has a subject.

Catch that man. (<u>You</u> **catch** that man.)
Is <u>your confidence</u> at a low ebb?
<u>The drug pusher</u> **was arrested** while drinking in The Slug and Lettuce.

A long sequence of simple sentences would be very monotonous but used sensitively they can be very effective indeed.

The simple sentences in the text on Edward VIII's abdication speech opposite are printed in bold type.

Edward VIII's Speech to the Nation

At long last I am able to say a few words of my own. I have never wanted to withhold anything but until now it has not been constitutionally possible for me to speak.

A few hours ago I discharged my last duty as King and Emperor, and now that I have been succeeded by my brother, the Duke of York, my first words must be to declare my allegiance to him. **This I do with all my heart.**

You all know the reasons which have impelled me to renounce the throne but I want you to understand that in making up my mind I did not forget the Country or the Empire which as Prince of Wales, and lately as King, I have for twenty-five years tried to serve. You must believe me when I tell you that I have found it impossible to carry the heavy burden of responsibility and to discharge my duties as King as I would wish without the help and support of the woman I love.

I now quit altogether public affairs and I lay down my burden. It may be some time before I return to my native land, but I shall always follow the fortunes of the British race and Empire with profound interest, and if at any time in the future I can be found to be of service to His Majesty in a private station I shall not fail. **And now we all have a new King. I wish him and you, his people, happiness and prosperity with all my heart. God bless you all. God save the King.**

The measured cadences of this prepared text and the solemnity of tone are entirely suited to the momentous occasion. It is this sensitivity in adapting your style to the occasion and to your audience that you should cultivate.

We are particularly concerned with sentence structure in this chapter and we shall be examining the contribution that variety in sentence construction can make. You will be encouraged to experiment with different sentence patterns and I hope you will relish the different effects that can be achieved. You will find that the possible combinations are endless and you will see why serious writers draft and redraft almost obsessively.

Don't expect to be able to write fluently and effectively without taking pains. I'm not suggesting you rewrite a letter of application for a job or a coursework essay many times but your letter and your essay will probably benefit from three or four attempts at rewording and polishing. When you re-read your first draft, you will see all sorts of opportunities for rephrasing this, rearranging that and clarifying this point and emphasising that. Not only is it worth rewriting from the point of view of getting a higher grade ('Does the candidate's style give pleasure?' is one of the questions examiners and moderators ask themselves) but it is also a deeply satisfying exercise. 'Language is the naming of experience,' writes Sir John Kingman, who chaired a committee of enquiry into the teaching of the English Language in 1988, 'and what we name we have power over.'

I hope you will enjoy the acquisition as well as the exercise of that power.

Compound sentences

Two or more simple sentences joined by co-ordinating conjunctions form a compound sentence.

> I now quit altogether public affairs **and** I lay down my burden.
> I like you very much **and** I respect you **but** I cannot marry you.

Useful co-ordinating conjunctions for forming compound sentences:

and	but then
and so	not only . . . but also
and then	or
both . . . and	either . . . or
as well as	neither . . . nor
but	

Exercise 61

Use appropriate co-ordinating conjunctions to combine these groups of simple sentences in the most effective way.

1) I do not know. I do not care.
2) She's a part-time teacher. She's a part-time physiotherapist.
3) Shall we have beef? Shall we have lamb?
4) You put down a deposit for the flat now. You lose the flat.
5) I shall go to the ball. I don't want to.

Exercise 62

Break down this passage into ten separate simple sentences without omitting any of the information.

I was deeply apprehensive at the prospect and I didn't mind admitting it, but he wouldn't listen to me. He was blind to my lack of basic survival skills and he was utterly convinced of my eligibility to be a team member. In fact, as well as being afraid of heights, I could neither swim nor canoe, and I was on the verge of a nervous breakdown. He swept every objection aside.

Exercise 63

Reduce these pairs of sentences to simple sentences by replacing verbs with nouns.

e.g. <u>You have been successful.</u> It will delight your parents.
     Your success will delight your parents.

You will have to make small modifications to the second sentence in most cases, as in the example above.

1) I do appreciate it. <u>You have been very kind.</u>

2) <u>I am coming to the end of my speech.</u> I must issue a general warning.

3) I must know. <u>Where are you going?</u>

4) <u>The child was distressed.</u> It was clear to everyone.

5) The committee listened gravely. <u>The Sanitary Engineer told them what should be done.</u>

Phrases and clauses

A phrase is a group of words which doesn't contain a finite verb and therefore doesn't make complete sense by itself:

running at top speed
with a ridiculous expression
to my great distress

A clause is a group of words which contains a finite verb. **Main clauses** *can* make complete sense on their own, but there are some cases where they are incomplete. A simple sentence is one main clause; a compound sentence has two or more main clauses.

Subordinate clauses are grammatically less important than main clauses. They supply additional information:

I stopped in my tracks (main clause)
because I heard a noise (subordinate clause)

Complex sentences

A complex sentence has one main clause and any number of subordinate clauses joined to it by subordinating conjunctions, and relative pronouns and adjectives:

You must believe me (main clause)
when **I tell you** (subordinate clause)
that **I have found it impossible**
to carry the heavy burden of
responsibility and to discharge
my duties as King without the
help and support of the woman (subordinate clause)
(whom) **I love** (subordinate clause)
as **I would wish** (subordinate clause)

Complex sentences are fun because by rearranging the order of the subordinate clauses you can gain a quite different emphasis.

Subordinate adverbial clauses

Some subordinate clauses do the work of adverbs; others do the work of nouns and adjectives.

Just as there are different kinds of adverbs, so there are different kinds of adverbial phrases and adverbial clauses:

He looked at me **contemptuously**. (adverb of manner)
He looked at me **with contempt**.
(adverbial phrase of manner)
He looked at me **as though he despised me**.
(adverbial clause of manner)

The names of the different kinds of adverbial clauses (e.g. adverbial clause of manner) don't really matter but I've given them below because the names are descriptive and they give you a good idea of the range of work that adverbial clauses do:

Time	Please come **when you can.**
	whenever you can.
	after you've finished lunch.
	before I go to bed.
	as the clock strikes nine.
	while it is still light.
	It has been lonely **since you left.**
	Wait for me **until you hear an owl hoot.**
Place	Put the note **where he will see it.**
	wherever he is sure to see it.
Manner	You look **as if you've seen a ghost.**
	as though you've seen a ghost.
	Roll out the pastry **as I've shown you.**
Reason	The train was cancelled **because it was foggy.**
	as it was foggy.
	since it was foggy.
Purpose	I put the glasses away **lest they got broken.**
	so that they would not get broken.
	in order that they would not get broken.
Degree	James is much taller **than you are.**
	Come as soon **as you can.**
Condition	I will come **if I can.**
	unless it rains.
	provided it doesn't rain.
Concession	Simon passed his exams **although he was careless.**
	even though he was careless.
	though he was careless.
Result	It was so hot **that we all collapsed.**

Exercise 64

Supply the adverbial clauses.

Jill knew that she had very little chance of getting the job **because** _____ . **As** _____ , she gave a wry grin. She had given up her teaching post **when** _____ . **If** _____ , she would probably be Head of Department by now. **Although** _____ , she felt a stab of resentment at the system. She had stopped teaching **so that** _____ **when** _____ and now it was probably too late to resume her career. **Although** _____ , she decided to post the application form **before** _____ .

Exercise 65

Use a subordinating conjunction of your choice to join each pair of sentences.

1) I cannot laugh. I am waiting for my face pack to dry.
2) It's very small. It's pretty.
3) You want to raise money. Do a parachute jump.
4) Helen Derwent bought her return ticket. She checked the train times carefully.
5) The mysterious stranger finished his soup. He pulled a gun from his pocket.

Exercise 66

Use these adverbial clauses in sentences of your own.

1) because he had such smelly feet.

2) even if I could eat a cabbage a day.

3) unless you prefer Portugal.

4) as I have shown you.

5) where Gloria can't see it.

Subordinate adjectival clauses

Subordinate adjectival clauses tell us more about nouns or pronouns just as adjectives and adjectival phrases do:

> He is a **famous** writer.   (adjective)
> He is a writer **of some renown**.   (adjectival phrase)
> He is a writer **who is well-known**.   (adjectival clause)

The relative pronouns **who**, **whom**, **which**, **that**, and the relative adjective **whose** join adjectival clauses to the main clause or to another subordinate clause:

> She is a lady **who knows me well**.
> She is a lady **whom I have known for years**.
> *She is a lady **I have known for years**.
> He is a novelist **whose books are bestsellers**.
> They gave me the book **that I had always wanted**.
> They gave me the book **which I had always wanted**.
> *They gave me the book **I had always wanted**.

*Sometimes **whom** and **which/that** are omitted but are 'understood'.

Sometimes joining two statements with **who**, **whom**, **whose**, **that**, **which** can involve considerable rearrangement. You need to decide which noun or pronoun the new adjectival clause describes and then place it immediately afterwards:

> Charles has fifty pence a week pocket-money. His father is a millionaire.
> Charles **whose** father is a millionaire has fifty pence a week pocket-money.

Remember who, whom and whose refer to people; that, which and whose refer to things

Exercise 67

Look closely at the adjectival clauses in bold type and say to which noun or pronoun they refer.

1) Even my godmother, **who has the sweetest nature imaginable**, lost her temper with the manager of the carpet shop.

2) The examination **which will be in the General Purpose** Hall will finish at 5 p.m.

3) Anyone **who has ever lived** in a village will know how expensive it can be.

4) The author **whom you praised so warmly** is being sued for libel.

5) Tania admitted ruefully that the earrings **she had bought** were very expensive.

6) Hardy was a man **who cared for such things**.

7) The meal **you cooked tonight** was marvellous.

8) The Howitts are people **who will always help in a crisis**.

9) I fear that my sister **who has behaved strangely for some time** is seriously ill.

10) The excuse **that you have given me** is simply not good enough.

Exercise 68

Use these adjectival clauses to describe a noun or pronoun in sentences of your own.

1) who has the most amazing memory of all
2) which was not entirely unexpected
3) that Joe Morris had wanted to buy for some time
4) (which) you gave me
5) whose pet rabbit escaped last Tuesday
6) whom you saw peering through my window
7) who had lunch with the Queen
8) who broke both legs
9) (whom) I met on holiday
10) that I took back to the shop

Exercise 69

Join each pair of sentences by using **whose**.

1) Eleanor is still very upset. Her cat was run over last weekend.

2) *Robinson Crusoe* is an eighteenth-century novel. Its opening sentence immediately captures the reader's attention.

3) *Syndrome* is a noun. Its meaning always eludes me.

4) It is a verdict. Its effects will be far-reaching.

5) Our neighbours are on holiday in France and know nothing about it. Their house was burnt down yesterday.

6) I'm looking for a bed. Its overall length is more than six foot.

7) No one will fail to believe in ghosts. His house has been haunted.

8) This is the friend. You met his wife in Bangkok.

9) The mother is a professional dressmaker. Her child won the fancy-dress competition.

10) Peter has few possessions. His peace of mind is enviable.

Subordinate Noun clauses

Noun clauses do all the jobs in a sentence that a noun or a noun phrase can do:

Subject

Fitness is an obsession with him.   (noun)

How to keep fit is an obsession with him.   (noun phrase)

That he must keep fit is an obsession with him.

(noun clause)

To find the subject, put WHO? or WHAT? in front of the verb

What is an obsession with him?

fitness √
how to keep fit √
that he must keep fit √

Object

He admires **fitness**.   (noun)

He knows **how to keep fit**.   (noun phrase)

He knows **that he must keep fit**.   (noun clause)

To find the object (if there is one), put WHOM? WHAT? after the verb

He admires **what**?   fitness √
He knows **what**?   how to keep fit √
He knows **what**?   that he must keep fit √

Complement

It is **exercise** that you need.   (noun)

This is **how to exercise**.   (noun phrase)

It seems **that you should exercise**.   (noun clause)

A small group of verbs take complements rather than objects to complete their sense. You need not concern yourself unduly with this but it does explain the expression you may have heard: 'The verb **to be** cannot take an object'.

To be, to seem, to become, to appear, to remain can all be followed by complements (nouns, pronouns or adjectives). If they are, they always refer back to the subject.

It is **I**. (not me, an *object* pronoun!)
Paul wants to become **an accountant**.
You seem **tired**.

Following a preposition

He is obsessed with **fitness**.   (noun)
He is obsessed with **keeping fit**.   (noun phrase)
He was impressed with **what you told him**.   (noun clause)

In apposition

His obsession, <u>fitness</u>, will be the death of him.   (noun)
His obsession, <u>keeping fit</u>, will be the death of him.
(noun phrase)
His obsession, <u>that he must be fit</u>, will be the death of him.
(noun clause)
It is his obsession <u>that he must be fit</u>.   (noun clause)

The phrase, **in apposition**, may need some explanation. In the sentences above, the words underlined can be substituted for the words in bold type. The second noun, noun phrase, or noun clause is said to be in apposition to the first noun or pronoun.

Exercise 70

Use these noun clauses in sentences of your own, using the examples on page 83 as a guide.

1) How she had managed to keep her marriage a secret for so long   (subject)
2) why you are so nervous   (object)
3) that he is to marry the boss's daughter   (complement)
4) when term ends   (following a preposition)
5) that she would emigrate   (in apposition)

Exercise 71

Write these sentences more concisely by substituting a noun for the noun clause in bold type.

1) We do not know **what he intends** to do.

   We do not know his _____ .

2) **That the match will be cancelled** now seems a certainty.

   The _____ of the match now seems a certainty.

3) Make a summary of **what was proposed**.

   Make a summary of the _____ .

4) Adrian told me **where he was**.

   Adrian told me his _____ .

5) Nobody could anticipate **that she would react like that**.

   Nobody could anticipate such a _____ .

6) I will never forget **how she behaved**.

   I will never forget her _____ .

7) **That the Chancellor of the Exchequer has been dismissed** was front-page news in every newspaper.

The _____ of the Chancellor of the Exchequer was front-page news in every newspaper.

8) **That you have delayed** may lose you the job.

Your _____ may lose you the job.

9) The store detective was fully aware of **what they had planned**.

The store detective was fully aware of their _____ .

10) The rumour **that they had eloped** spread quickly.

The rumour of their _____ spread quickly.

Synthesis and compression

Exercise 72

Write up these notes on Charlotte Bronte using not more than three well-constructed sentences. (To make the exercise a little more difficult, avoid using **and**, **but**, **or**!) You can rearrange the order.

Bronte Charlotte (1816–55) – novelist – daughter of Revd Patrick Bronte – village of Haworth – parsonage overlooked cemetery – on Yorkshire Moors – mother died when Charlotte a child – two younger sisters, Emily and Anne, both wrote novels – brother, Branwell, very talented artist but drank heavily – married Revd A. Nicholls in 1854 – died 1855 – *Jane Eyre* published

1847, *Shirley* in 1849 and *Villette* in 1852 – her first novel *The Professor* published after her death.

Exercise 73

Write out this recipe, using three well-constructed sentences. (By the way, it's a good recipe.)

Good recipe for flapjacks – very large Swiss roll tin needed, approximately 40 × 30 cm – mixture makes sixty flapjacks – 300 g butter or margarine – 150 g demerara sugar – 150 g golden syrup – 400 g quick porridge oats – pinch of salt – melt butter gently in a saucepan – add all other ingredients – stir thoroughly – remove from heat – turn mixture into greased Swiss roll tin – spread smoothly – bake for about half an hour – middle of moderate oven – gas mark 4, 375 °F – allow to cool – cut into sixty fingers.

Direct and indirect speech

There will be times when you will want to use direct speech in your writing. Direct speech is when the actual words of a speaker are quoted.

'What is that gun firing for?' said Boxer.
'To celebrate our victory!' cried Squealer.
'What victory?' said Boxer. His knees were bleeding, he had lost a shoe and split his hoof, and a dozen pellets had lodged themselves in his hindleg.
'What victory, comrade? Have we not driven the enemy

off our soil – the sacred soil of Animal Farm?'

'But they have destroyed the windmill. And we had worked on it for two years!'

'What matter? We will build another windmill. We will build six windmills if we feel like it. You do not appreciate, comrade, the mighty thing that we have done. The enemy was in occupation of this very ground that we stand upon. And now – thanks to the leadership of Comrade Napoleon – we have won every inch of it back again!'

'Then we have won back what we had before,' said Boxer.

'That is our victory,' said Squealer.

George Orwell, Animal Farm (Methuen, 1985)

Both Squealer and Boxer tell us a great deal about themselves while talking of other things. A skilful writer by capturing special patterns of speech accurately can present characters very vividly to us. Notice also how both characters in the extract from *Animal Farm* are helping the story substantially as they talk. Direct speech in *less* skilful hands can actually hold the story up, weary the reader, and tell us nothing at all about the speaker. Below is a taste of the idle conversation that one often meets in the work of students.

'That will be ninety-five pence, please.' I gave her a pound note.

'Thank you. Five pence change.'

'Thank you very much. Goodbye.'

'Goodbye.'

Very often indirect speech is more appropriate than direct speech. Indirect speech is the reporting (and often the summarising) of what has been spoken. It enables the writer to be concise and to be relevant and to isolate the significance of what is said.

Then she began to say openly that she did not feel well, that the house was too much for her, and that the doctor had imperatively commanded rest. She said this to everybody

> except Mardon. And everybody somehow persisted in not
> saying it to Mardon.
>
> Arnold Bennett *The Old Wives' Tale* (Pan Books, 1979)

You see how much Arnold Bennett is able to convey in 45 words. Indirect speech can be very concise indeed while ranging freely over time and space.

Indirect speech does not come naturally. It requires conscious shaping and a measure of detachment.

Let us consider the changes that need to be made when direct speech is converted to indirect speech while omitting nothing. When you have practised converting one to the other, you will enjoy the freedom of using whichever is most appropriate at any point in your own work.

Look closely at these two sentences and note the changes which take place when direct speech is converted to indirect speech:

'I shall finish the painting today,' I insisted.

He insisted **that he would** finish the painting **that day**.

You will see that everything is written at one remove: **I** becomes **he**; tenses are written one tense further back in time; **today** becomes **that day**.

Try your hand at converting a passage of direct speech to indirect speech before we go into these changes more fully. Detailed advice will be seen as more relevant when you have met some of the difficulties.

Exercise 74

Rewrite as indirect speech, without omitting any of the information given. Begin: Mrs Pront grumbled that it was . . .

'What a bitterly cold Easter!' exclaimed Mrs Pront. 'We had planned to take the caravan to North Devon but it's too cold for the outdoor life. Don't you agree?'

'It's the worst Easter I've known,' nodded Mrs Green. 'Still my daughter comes tomorrow with the seven grandchildren. I shall have my hands so full that I won't notice the weather!'

Direct to indirect speech

You make these changes. (They look complicated but most are made instinctively once you get going!)

Pronouns
Change all personal pronouns to the third person (to he/him, she/her, they/them).

Direct speech	*Indirect speech*
I, me	he/she, him/her
you (singular)	he/she, him/her
we, us	they/them
you (plural)	they/them

Tenses
Indirect speech is usually written in the past tense, whereas direct speech is written from a standpoint in the present. Move every tense back in time. (Present becomes past, future becomes future in the past.)

Direct speech	Indirect speech
he sleeps	he slept
he is sleeping	he was sleeping
he has slept	he had slept
he has been sleeping	he had been sleeping
he will sleep	he would sleep
he will be sleeping	he would be sleeping
he will have slept	he would have slept
he will have been sleeping	he would have been sleeping

Adverbs referring to time and place

Direct speech	Indirect speech
now	then
today	that day
tomorrow	the next day/the day after
yesterday	the previous day/the day before
the day before yesterday	two days before
next week	the following week
ago	before
here	there
this place	that place

Verbs of saying

Introduce statements, questions, and commands with an appropriate verb of **saying**. Some useful verbs follow. (You will be able to add to the list.)

Statements

These verbs will be followed by **that** or **how**: admit, assert, affirm, believe, claim, hope, promise, reply, retort, say, state, whisper.

Questions

These verbs will be followed by **if** or **whether**: ask, enquire, want to know, wonder.

Commands
These verbs will be followed by **that** or the infinitive: **advise,
beg, command, entreat, implore, invite, order, recommend,
remind, request, suggest, tell, urge, warn.**

Exclamations and short phrases
Exclamations and short phrases can often be neatly replaced
by a verb of saying:

'I am sorry,' she said.
She apologised.

'Good heavens!' he exclaimed.
He expressed surprise.

'Good morning, sir,' said the boy.
'Good morning!' snapped the teacher.
**The boy greeted his teacher politely but was met by a
brusque response.**

Ambiguity

Ambiguity is a constant danger in indirect speech with its high proportion of third person pronouns:

Direct speech   'Why didn't you wait until I was better?' asked John.

Indirect speech   John asked him why he hadn't waited until **he** was better. (**Who was better?**)

Be alert to the danger and you will find ways of avoiding confusion to the reader. One rather clumsy remedy is to insert a name in brackets after the confusing pronoun:

> John asked him why he hadn't waited until he (**John**) was better.

In other contexts, it is often possible to introduce a proper noun in place of the pronoun:

> John asked Mr Thompson where **his** son was. (**John's son? Mr Thompson's son?**)
>
> √   John asked Mr Thompson where Mr Thompson's son was.
>
> √√   John asked Mr Thompson where Kevin was.

Exercise 75

Rewrite as indirect speech. Don't summarise on this occasion. Aim to include everything.

'What do you have for homework, tonight?' Mrs Baines asked her daughter.

'We've got four subjects and they've all got to be handed in tomorrow,' moaned Sharon.

Mrs Baines felt sorry for her daughter but she concealed this and approached the problem more practically.

'Well,' she said, 'get two subjects done before supper and you'll be half way there.'

'Huh!' snorted the thirteen-year-old, unimpressed by this solution.

Exercise 76

Rewrite as direct speech. Try to write what you think the characters actually said.

The manager apologised profusely and claimed that he had never had any complaints about the workmanship of that particular product before. Mrs Greening listened to all this rather impatiently before countering with a request for her money back. He agreed immediately but couldn't resist apologising all over again.

Exercise 77

Rewrite this exchange from Oscar Wilde's *The Importance of Being Earnest* as indirect speech. Try to preserve the flavour as much as you can.

Lady Bracknell	(*sitting down*) You can take a seat, Mr Worthing. (*looks in her pocket for note-book and pencil*)
Jack	Thank you, Lady Bracknell. I prefer standing.

| Lady Bracknell | (*pencil and notebook in hand*) I feel bound to tell you that you are not down on my list of eligible young men, although I have the same list as the dear Duchess of Bolton has. We work together, in fact. However I am quite ready to enter your name, should your answers be what a really affectionate mother requires. Do you smoke? |
| Jack | Well, yes. I must admit I smoke. |

Oscar Wilde, The Importance of Being Earnest
(Penguin)

Exercise 78

Rewrite this extract from *Cider with Rosie* as indirect speech. Try to keep the tone of the original.

The morning came, without any warning, when my sisters surrounded me, wrapped me in scarves, tied up my bootlaces, thrust a cap on my head, and stuffed a baked potato in my pocket.

'What's this?' I said.

'You're starting school today.'

'I ain't. I'm stopping 'ome.'

'Now, come on, Loll. You're a big boy now.

'I ain't.'

'You are.'

'Boo-hoo.'

They picked me up bodily, kicking and bawling, and carried me up the road.

'Boys who don't go to school get put into boxes, and turn into rabbits, and get chopped up on Sundays.'

I felt this was overdoing it rather, but I said no more after that.

Laurie Lee, Cider with Rosie (Penguin, 1983)

Exercise 79

In small groups, read the newspaper article which follows.

1) Rewrite Charles Chapman's quoted words as indirect speech. Do you think direct or indirect speech is more appropriate? Why?

2) Rewrite the penultimate paragraph as direct speech. Why do you think Coky Giedroyc decided not to use direct speech here?

Poll tax ploy
by Coky Giedroyc

A retired docker living in the village of St Dominick, Cornwall, has renamed his bungalow Alfresco Abbey, and has declared himself a monk, in order to avoid the Poll Tax charges due to replace domestic rates next April. Some religious houses will be exempt from the new charge.

Charles Chapman, 58, better known, of late, as Brother Charles, said, 'I am a Christian, but this new order has no rules, regulations or committees. The motto is: don't upset anyone else, and have a sense of humour.' Unperturbed by suggestions that he become celibate and have no income, Mr Chapman explained, 'I couldn't find anything in the dictionary to say I have to do all that. There's nothing to say I can't declare myself a monk. Besides, I've got plenty of Bibles and hymn books here and a couple of wooden crosses, too.'

Mr Chapman, who is living on invalidity benefit after heart surgery, believes that he can save £200 by formally registering his home as a monastery with local Caradon District Council. In return, he has promised to pray and sing hymns.

'Lots of people are approaching me to join the order,' he said. 'If they ask me how to meditate, I tell them to watch England in the Test Match.'

The Catholic Herald, 2 June 1989

Exercise 80

Write Robert de Baudricourt's brief entry in his journal describing his 'conversation' with his steward. Use no more than 20 words to summarise the exchange and his reaction to it.

Robert de Baudricourt	No eggs! No eggs! Thousand thunders, man, what do you mean by no eggs?
Steward	Sir, it is not my fault. It is the act of God.
Robert de Baudricourt	Blasphemy. You tell me there are no eggs; and you blame your Maker for it.
Steward	Sir, what can I do? I cannot lay eggs.
Robert de Baudricourt	(*sarcastic*) Ha! You jest about it.
Steward	No, sir. God knows we all have to go without eggs just as you have, sir. The hens will not lay.

George Bernard Shaw, *St Joan* (Penguin)

Chapter Three

PARAGRAPHS

This section is written for all students who find that paragraphing is a bewildering exercise. I know that many find it so, for I have met students who confess they paragraph on an entirely random basis; they start a new paragraph whenever the last one 'looks long enough' or they indent every eight or nine lines in the interests of symmetry whether a division at that point in the text is appropriate or not. Others never attempt to paragraph and yet others play safe and start a new paragraph with every new sentence.

This confusion is entirely unnecessary. Paragraphing is logical. It is not random; it is not mysterious; it is not difficult.

You need to know what you want to say before you start writing. If you want to make five separate points about your subject then you write about each in a separate paragraph; the introduction and the conclusion will each be another paragraph and so you will have seven paragraphs altogether. As a very rough guide, a 400 word essay would probably have five or six paragraphs (introduction and conclusion and three or four substantial paragraphs in between) but one can't generalise. Until you've planned what you want to say, you don't know how many paragraphs you will need.

In my experience, it is those students who have not planned in advance what they are going to say who have difficulty in paragraphing a letter, an essay, an article or a short story. It's not necessary to make a very elaborate plan – you don't even have to write it down – but you do need to know what each of your paragraphs is going to be about.

Paragraphs can be any length. A paragraph can be one sentence but too many one-sentence paragraphs in a row might be rather tedious. At the other extreme, a paragraph which threatens to become longer than one side of A4 paper may well benefit from being broken into a number of shorter paragraphs each embodying separate subsidiary points.

Paragraphing is really the visual presentation of the logical structure of a piece of writing.

Headings and subheadings in business documents and leaflets and handbooks, often make the structure of the text absolutely clear and make it very easy for the reader to find the information he wants. These headings and subheadings are themselves the *plan* of the document. You could write an excellent essay or article dealing with the topics in the order given on just such lines.

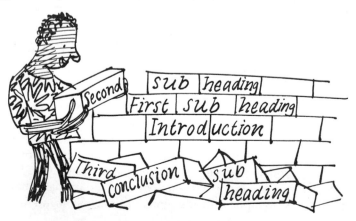

TUNING ON THE WATER

Balance

It is most important to find out if the boat is *balanced* (i.e. goes straight when sailed dead upright). To do so, sail the boat on a beat, making sure that it is level and that both sails are trimmed; the helmsman then puts his tiller hand over and around the tiller without touching it (but ready to correct immediately if need be). In medium winds the boat should go straight ahead without any tiller correction. If the boat turns into the wind, move the mast step forward, keeping the rake constant. If the mast step is already as far forward as the rules of measurement allow, reduce the aft rake of the mast. When beating upwind most helmsmen like to feel a 'pull' on the tiller ('weather helm') – remember that this is added drag, reducing upwind speed.

Halyards

Performance upwind is often lost by the main halyard stretching or slipping so that the gaff falls away from the mast. The tension on the . . .

Roy Partridge, Sailing the Mirror (Fernhurst Books)

This snippet from a section on tuning in a handbook on sailing shows how useful subheadings can be in dividing up a text for easy reference. However, consider what an excellent plan the subheadings in the section provide for an essay or article. (You would have to add a conclusion.)

Tuning

What is tuning?

       Tuning on land – mast rake
                   – shrouds and forestay
                   – jib
                   – mainsail
       Tuning on water – balance
                   – halyards
                   – sail controls

Sir Ernest Gowers in *The Complete Plain Words* (Penguin, 1987) defines a paragraph as 'a unit of thought not of length ... homogeneous in subject matter, and sequential in treatment of it'. This puts it in a nutshell, even if rather forbiddingly, and I hesitate to paraphrase. You may like to define a paragraph for yourself after examining a number of them.

Exercise 81

Suggest the sub-headings which you think the writers used to summarise the content of each of these paragraphs. Answers are at back of book.

1) If a doe scatters her youngsters over the hutch floor, and seems to take no interest in them, it is sometimes possible to save them if they can be found before they get too chilled. They should be put in a box lined with some warm materials and put in a warm room fairly near the fire. They can do without food for twenty-four hours, but they cannot do without warmth. The cause of a doe neglecting her young is often because her milk supply has not begun to function. If the milk comes within a few hours of the birth of the litter, as it frequently does, the youngsters can be returned to the nest and the doe will soon begin to look after them. Maiden does are more likely to scatter their youngsters than experienced does.

C. F. Snow, *Rabbit Keeping* (Foyles Handbook)

2) The simplest of the ready-made barbecues is the Hibachi style of grill. This was first developed in Japan and hibachi is the Japanese word for fire bowl. It is an extremely compact barbecue, eminently suited for use in the garden, for picnics and for camping and caravanning holidays. It has a solid cast iron or steel fire bowl with vents and grills and several cooking levels. Choose from two or three grill models with small squat feet for use on the ground or on a small stone or metal table; alternatively, choose a round single grill model with a centre leg and wheels.

Judy Ridgway, *Barbecues* (Ward Lock, 1983)

3) There are a few simple rules to be observed. Firstly, when taking plaster off the hawk remember to move the hawk with the trowel in the direction of the wall or surface being worked on. Push the plaster on to the wall, using a fair degree of pressure, and gradually flatten the trowel towards the surface as the plaster is spread. Keep the trowel slightly on edge so that it is not quite in the same plane as the wall. If it is tilted too much it will scrape rather than spread the plaster and is likely to result in a series of wavy lines. If it is too flat it will tend to stick to the plaster by suction. If the thickness of old plaster which the patch must match is not too great it may be possible to carry out the repair with one coat of plaster. If not, two coats must be applied. The finishing coat should be quite thin and applied as soon as the first coat has set. Keep the surface of the trowel wet.

G. C. A. Tanner, *House Maintenance and Repairs* (Penguin, 1965)

The topic sentences in the next three examples are underlined.

A paragraph explores one topic, as you have seen, and very often (as in the middle paragraph in the last exercise), you will find one sentence (often called **the topic sentence**) which sums up what the paragraph is about. The topic sentence is frequently the opening sentence of a paragraph but it can be delayed very effectively until the middle of the paragraph or even until the end.

Another sloppy posture which sometimes becomes a habit is taking the weight on one leg. This action reduces the total muscular effort of standing erect and puts a stretch on the ligaments of the leg which takes the weight and on the lower spinal ligaments. If the habit of standing on one leg is always to the same side those ligaments eventually protest and hurt but also there is a risk that a spinal curvature will develop. When prolonged standing is unavoidable it is safe enough to stand on one leg for a while, but swing over to the other side and give the first leg a rest too.

Dr Alan Stoddard, *The Back* (Macdonald Optima, 1979)

Decisions . . . decisions. You probably feel beset by them, and although there are many good sources of advice from school, college and the local careers service, and information from reference books and prospectuses, it takes time to reach a decision. But decisions about what and where to study are really quite important because they are going to affect you for the rest of your life. Some sixth-formers and college students have very definite ideas about what they want to do. Some want to go to university – and will not consider anything else: some even plan on aiming for just one university! Others may refuse to contemplate at all the idea of going on to a full-time course after A-levels. If you are in one of these categories beware – you could find yourself with real problems after the results come out.

Brian Heap, Degree Course Offers 1990 (Trotman & Co, 1989)

Hitler is now sprawled over Europe. Our offensive springs are being slowly compressed, and we must resolutely and methodically prepare ourselves for the campaigns of 1941 and 1942. Two or three years are not a long time, even in our precarious lives. They are nothing in the history of the nation, and when we are doing the finest thing in the world, and have the honour to be the sole champion of the liberties of all Europe, we must not grudge these years or weary as we toil and struggle through them. It does not follow that our energies in future years will be exclusively confined to defending ourselves and our possessions. Many opportunities may lie open to amphibious power, and we must be ready to take advantage of them. One of the ways to bring this war to a speedy end is to convince the enemy, not by words, but by deeds, that we have both the will and the means, not only to go on indefinitely but to strike heavy and unexpected blows. The road to victory may not be so long as we expect. But we have no right to count upon this. Be it long or short, rough or smooth, we mean to reach our journey's end.

Speech to the House of Commons
Sir Winston Churchill, 20 August 1940

Exercise 82

Find the topic sentences in the five paragraphs below.

1) Lunch with Sir John does not only bring back what, to some, may seem the vanishing magic of the pre-war West End, but also the Victorian theatre aristocracy of which Gielgud was a child. His grandmother, Kate Terry, played Ophelia, Juliet, Beatrice and Portia before settling down in a large house on Campden Hill with Arthur Lewis, a fashionable haberdasher who organized evenings with a Glee Club and kept a cow for fresh milk somewhere near Holland Avenue. Kate was the eldest of the family of Terrys which included Fred, who created the Scarlet Pimpernel and went on playing that role though crippled with gout, Marion, who played the shady Mrs Erlynne in *Lady Windermere's Fan*, and, above all, Ellen. Gielgud remembers Ellen Terry as an old lady, swathed in shawls and crowned with a huge black hat, unable to recollect lines or which was which among her vast crowd of nephews and nieces. She beckoned the young John to her and said, 'Which are you and do you read your Shakespeare?"

John Mortimer, *In Character* (Penguin, 1984)

2) Patrick Stewart:
I once understudied Falstaff and I was very privileged to watch an actor rehearse that part and then play it for a long Stratford season, an actor who for me has explored that character more fully than anyone else, and that was Paul Rogers. What I learnt about Falstaff through watching him was that there is, beside that energetic, turbulent, wilful, humorous spirit in Falstaff, a man who is small, narrow, mean, grotesquely selfish and self-centred, wicked and cruel, and I thought that he developed those two strands in the character extraordinarily well. There were always reasons why he did things – why he would take so much stick from Hal and the others, because it benefited him; and why he would finally abandon everyone and everything in order to save himself. One often hears of Falstaff, or sees him, being a kind of Father Christmas figure – a benevolent,

jolly character – and I think it's important to find those vicious and violent elements in the man because they help to set off what is so funny and enjoyable about him.

Myra Barrs (ed.), Shakespeare Superscribe (Penguin, 1980)

3) Gopal and his bride were sitting on the stage, the guru chanting in front of them. Guests filed past, paying their respects and laying gifts on the floor. 'You see the shrine, that's where people make offerings of food to the gods.' Sally heard the word food, saw where Sandya was pointing, and was off, up the side steps, past the astonished guru and the beflowered bride and groom. Happily, the little girl began tucking into the food of the gods. Nuts, sweets, candies were consumed before Sumitra, positioned behind the bride, realized what was going on and hurriedly caught her up. Sally was passed along from hand to hand, back to Maria. All the guests, the guru, the bridge and groom began to laugh. Sally buried her head in Maria's neck and sobbed. One of the women hastily brought a plate of jalabi and offered it to the child. Sally gave a damp smile and began to eat.

Rukshana Smith, Sumitra's Story (Bodley Head)

4) The striking difference between us and our forebears in the last and every preceding generation is that we are far less physically active. Our grandparents couldn't so much accuse us of the deadly sin of gluttony but rather of sloth. In our push-button, mechanised world we can get away with hardly moving our bodies at all if we don't want to. Even those of us who do manual work have far more machines to help us than the last generation. The rest of us expend very few calories in our day-to-day work and in our leisure time the only exercise we may get is flicking a finger at the remote control which changes channels on our television set!

Dr Barry Lynch, The BBC Diet (BBC Books, 1988)

5) Although the communication was made more than 24 hours ago, no reply has been received, but German attacks upon Poland have been continued and intensified. I have, accordingly, the honour to inform you that unless not later

than 11 a.m., British Summer Time, to-day, September 3rd, satisfactory assurances to the above effect have been given by the German Government and have reached His Majesty's Government in London, a state of war will exist between the two countries as from that hour.

Letter from Neville Chamberlain to German Foreign Secretary,
3 September 1939

Exercise 83

Arrange these sentences to form the best possible order within one paragraph.

1) It was a story which was repeated by many of the old people who lived nearby.

2) I remember one frail old lady who spoke movingly of his kindness to her during the blizzards that had cut off the town for weeks the year before.

3) Mr Blenheim was a man who had many grateful friends in the little, narrow-fronted houses that had huddled near his shop.

4) She described with tears in her eyes how he had visited her daily and claimed it was his concern that had kept her spirits up more than anything else which had been done by official social workers.

5) One man whom arthritis and rheumatism had reduced to near-helplessness told of gifts that were quietly given at intervals throughout the year.

Exercise 84

Read Philip Howard's article, noticing carefully how he has structured his case. Write the plan he might have used, summarising the topic of each paragraph as briefly as you can.

New names addressed

It is a wise parent whose children are satisfied with their Christian names. Most of us have fantasies that our lives would be improved if we were called something less plain if we are called Jane, or something more plain if we are called Aphrodite or Ebenezer.

Sam Goldwyn arrived in America with a Polish surname that was deemed unpronounceable by the immigration officers. So he adopted the name Goldfish. Goldwyn evolved as his name and the name of his movie company from an amalgamation of Goldfish and an early partner, Edgar Selwyn. A lawsuit was brought, challenging his right to use the invented name. In the course of the hearing the judge, who eventually ruled in Goldwyn's favour, observed: "A self-made man may prefer a self-made name."

There is a lot of self-made naming going on *Pamella* Bordes, the parliament researcher into the Net Book Agreement, put the second "l" in *Pamella* because it was different, and perhaps because it suggests the fashionable double-barrelled first name, making the best of two worlds: Sue-Ellen, Pam Ella.

Pamela itself was first used by Sir Philip Sidney in his *Arcadia* (1590). If he invented it, it is not clear quite what he meant by it, though a derivation from the two Greek words "all honey", i.e., all sweetness, is possible. Samuel Richardson brought the name into general use with Pamela Andrews, the heroine of his best-selling novel, *Pamela*, in 1740. In the 18th century pronunciation varied between Pameela and the modern Pamela. Peak popularity of Pamela in English-speaking countries was in the Fifties; the name has faded now.

Marilyn is another of these invented names getting the best of two names, Mary and Ellen. One of its earliest users was Marilyn Miller, the American musical star of the Twenties, originally named Mary Ellen Miller. In the Forties Marilyn Maxwell (christened Marvel Maxwell, poor kid) began to appear regularly on cinema screens. By now the name had reached Britain, and became very popular in the Fifties. Then came Marilyn Monroe (originally Norma Jean Baker or Mortenson), who was renamed by a casting agent with Marilyn Miller in mind. Since then it seems to me that the name has faded in popularity in Britain at least. Teachers are the people who are better placed than literary editors to keep closely in touch with changes of fashion in nomenclature.

Australian soaps that are beginning to lather our television screens are a rich source of brave new names, such as *Cheredith*, which I take to be another two-pronged name, combingng Cherry with Edith, by analogy with Meredith. On balance, I am quite relieved that my parents and godparents did not choose it for me. And what strange new name for girls is this *Kylie* Minogue, an actress from *Neighbours*? Jolly interesting, as it happens. It comes from *karli*, a name for a kind of boomerang in Nyungar and related languages of the Aborigines of Western Australia. It is recorded as early as 1835: "I am sorry that nasty word boomerang has been suffered to supercede [sic] the proper name. Boomerang is a corruption used at Sydney by the white people, but not the native word, which is tur-ra-ma; but *kiley* is the name here."

Kiley was adapted in transferred use to mean a small piece of board upon which two pennies are rested for spinning in an Australian game: "The game is played with two pennies, a mattress, a thin piece of wood called a kip (sometimes a stick or a *kiley*), and amazing dexterity and ardour." *Kylie*'s use as a girl's Christian name has been confined to Australia, at any rate until the arrival of *Neighbours* on our screens. It has interacted and mated with Kelly, the Irish surname used as a Christian name for both boys and girls in Australia. And *Kylie* was influenced by Grace Kelly, who played a leading role in the vastly popular and influential *High Society* (1956). The names of the tiresome character she portrayed in the film, Tracy Samantha, were also taken up from that time on. On such silken threads are new names spun.

We are continually making up new names. J.M. Barrie invented *Wendy* for *Peter Pan* in 1904, after a child had used the twee phrase "friendy-wendy" to him. In fact there were already several Germanic names in existence, such as *Wendelburg* and *Wendelgard*, which might have produced such a pet name less nauseatingly. The silly name has been helped along by three British actresses, *Wendy* Hiller, *Wendy* Barrie, and *Wendy* Craig. *Thelma* was invented by Marie Corelli for the heroine of her novel *Thelma* (1887), presumably based on the Greek *thelema*, will. *Thelma* Ritter, the comedienne, gave it a boost, but it has faded, and it is now quietly used, mostly by black American parents.

Fiona was invented as the first part of his pseudonym. *Fiona* Macleod, by William Sharp (1855–1905). It is derived from the Gaelic *fionn*, fair or white, became very popular in Scotland, reached a peak in England in the Seventics, but is not used in the United States. There are tides in the names of men, and particularly women; and they are shifting, pulled by the moon of fashion, all the time.

Philip Howard
The Times, 20 June 1989

Exercise 85

Read the editorial comment which appeared in *The Times* and *The Sun* the day after the 1989 Notting Hill Carnival.

1) What differences can you see in the two different styles of format and presentation?

2) What is the average sentence length of paragraphs in *The Sun* and paragraphs in *The Times*?

3) The tone of the two articles is very different. What makes it so?

4) What purpose do you think each editor had in writing his editorial?

5) Without changing *The Sun* text in any way, suggest where the text could be broken to make four paragraphs only.

THE CARNIVAL IS OVER

Immediate reactions to any trouble at the Notting Hill Carnival are even more predictable than the trouble itself. A long cool assessment of this year's violence is now necessary before any counter-measures are decided.

To call, for instance, for the annual festival to be stopped is to display a lack of realism. This is not to say that most residents of West London would not sigh with relief if such a permanent ban could be enacted. But so would those living near the flight path at Heathrow in the event of the airport being miraculously shifted.

The carnival is not as immovable as Heathrow. Indeed its future was seriously questioned two years ago following an effusion of unparalleled crime and violence. To try closing it down after 24 years, however, would probably cause more trouble than carrying on with it.

Nor would this be justified in the present circumstances. The aggression on Monday night came after two days of noisy but more or less peaceful pleasure-seeking. Without the trouble that began in All Saints Road, the success this year would have been unqualified.

What happened then seems to have been as follows. Called to deal with a disturbance in the area, the police were attacked with missiles and, in one case at least, a knife. Fearing an escalation to widespread rioting, they operated a contingency plan to clear the area, using riot shields for protection as they did so.

The issue which may never be resolved is whether such comprehensive tactics were correct. Leaders of the new Carnival Enterprise Committee have argued that, while the police had to take action, they did so in a heavy-handed manner. They contend that a little more patience and constraint would have been more appropriate and less provocative.

Perhaps with the benefit of hindsight they are right. The police certainly put at risk their public image, in the eyes of the black community at least, by ending what remained of this year's carnival.

But senior officers had to make a judgement on the spot, in what seemed at the time an explosive situation. With memories of Broadwater Farm still all too fresh, they opted not to risk a serious riot. Had the confrontation developed in this way, the police would almost certainly have been blamed.

On the success of this year's carnival until then, both the police and the enterprise committee are agreed. The crime rate and the number of arrests were both well down. The atmosphere was friendly and relaxed.

Moreover the police operation might equally be considered a success. That it seemed necessary at that moment was regrettable. But they proved that with 5,000 men and careful planning, they could cope with contingencies quickly and efficiently. Compared with some similar incidents in the past, this was quite a clean and surgical operation.

To argue, as some have tried to since the weekend, that the police should never have been there in the first place, is a nonsense. There might come a day when the enterprise committee will realize its dream of an event which is entirely self-policed. But that day is, at best, several years away.

If the annual Notting Hill Carnival is to flourish (and there is no real alternative to trying to make it do so) it must develop as an orderly event. If it is ever to contribute to better race relations (so far its impact has been largely detrimental) the committee and the police will have to work together, on the basis of mutual, instinctive understanding.

No event which draws up to half a million people in one day will ever be very easy to control. A certain amount of petty crime and drunkenness is almost a fact of life on such occasions, a demonstration of human fallibility.

For the most part, however, the new enterprise committee would seem to have made an encouraging beginning. Together with the police it has 12 more months in which to get next year's act together. Cool heads and careful judgement will be needed to avoid a return to excesses of the past.

The Times, 30 August 1989

The carnival MUST be over

HOME Secretary Douglas Hurd has called for reports on the violence at Notting Hill Carnival.

We know what this means. He will do precisely **NOTHING**.

Yet the time really has come to call an end to this annual exercise in mayhem.

The carnival begins in colour and fun.

But every year thugs turn it into an exercise in hatred and violence.

This time, 32 policemen were hurt in vicious street battles with missile throwing gangs.

The scale of the trouble is shown by arrests exceeding 300.

Around 5,000 police officers were deployed in Notting Hill over the weekend.

The cost to the public is put at a figure approaching £2 million.

Blood

The carnival organisers argue that the trouble is small in relation to the crowds.

Maybe. But it is still unacceptable.

Members of the black community also have the effrontery to suggest that the police presence was a "provocation" to black youths.

What do they want? Blood in the streets as thugs turn on defenceless men, women and children?

The 1989 Carnival should be the last. But definitely.

The Sun, 30 August 1989

Exercise 86

Write a description of someone you know well using this plan:

introduction

family background/education

appearance

temperament and personality

interests

ambitions

conclusion

110

ANSWERS

Exercise 3
Avenue, Meteor, Bristol, Friday, Lorna

Exercise 4
1) pride
2) generosity
3) depth
4) poverty
5) perseverance

Exercise 5
oxen
foxes
cities
women
turkeys
sopranos
princesses
mosquitoes
laboratories
handkerchiefs
mothers-in-law

Exercise 6
1) flock
2) herd
3) batch
4) galaxy, constellation
5) fleet
6) pride
7) shoal
8) anthology
9) litter
10) regiment, battalion, army, company, etc.

Exercise 9
Jobs and Careers after A-levels
situation
choice
job
interest
rejection
problems
education
mistake
criteria
opportunity

Exercise 10
1) me
2) me
3) me
4) me
5) me
6) me
7) I
8) me
9) I
10) me

Exercise 11
1, 3, 5, 10

Exercise 12

1) *Either*   If you are to look your best, you ...
   or   If one is to look one's best, one ...
2) *Either*   One never knows ... one should ...
   or   You never know ... you should ...
3) *Either*   A nurse ... tries ... she is bound ...
   or   Nurses ... try ... they are bound ...
4) *Either*   ... the housewife is ... I advise her ...
   or   ... housewives are ... I advise them ...
5) Each of them is ...
6) *Either*   You would ... you can ...
   or   One would ... one can ...
7) Each ... is equipped ...
8) *Either*   ... he should help his friends.
   or   ... one should help one's friends.
9) *Either*   Teachers ... their pupils ...
   or   A teacher ... his pupils ...
   or   A teacher ... her pupils ...
10) *Either*   ... one experiences ... one's early years has an effect on one ... one's life.
    or   ... you experience ... your early years has an effect on you ... your life.

Exercise 13

1) who
2) who
3) whom
4) who
5) whom
6) whom
7) whom
8) whom
9) whom
10) who

Exercise 14

1) who
2) whom
3) whom
4) who
5) who
6) whom
7) whom
8) who
9) whom
10) who

Exercise 17

1) hazard
2) teeth
3) week
4) nonsense
5) fillings
6) amalgam
7) fillings
8) teeth
9) materials
10) materials
11) materials
12) effects
13) ones
14) fillings
15) fillings
16) fillings
17) cause

Exercise 19

'On This Island', W. H. Auden

leaping
stable
silent
swaying

tall
sucking
sheer

floating
urgent
these

Exercise 20

1) Liverpudlian
2) Parisian
3) Manx
4) Slavonic
5) Norwegian
6) Danish
7) Neapolitan
8) Swiss
9) Dickensian
10) Georgian

Exercise 21

1) mountainous
2) circular
3) exemplary
4) parental
5) chaotic
6) choral
7) wise
8) troublesome
9) gigantic
10) conscientious

Exercise 22

1) sympathetic
2) sleepy
3) quarrelsome
4) favourite
5) ridiculous
6) explosive
7) pleasant
8) critical
9) inflammable
10) wakeful

Exercise 24

1) ... more generous
2) ... the loveliest ...
4) ... the longer
8) ... my favourite ...
9) ... more energetic ...
10) ... than any other magazine ...

Exercise 25

1) who's
2) whose
3) whose
4) whose
5) who's
6) who's
7) whose
8) who's
9) whose
10) who's

Exercise 26

1) It's
2) it's
3) its
4) It's
5) its
6) its
7) It's
8) It's
9) it's
10) It's

Exercise 27

1) telephoned
2) is
3) Hurry
4) seized ... shook
5) am ... frightened
6) spun ... left
7) strode ... flung ... jumped
8) swallowed ... fainted
9) miaowed ... purred ... saw
10) knelt ... took ... slipped

Exercise 28

1) Mrs Hallan (was), Sandra (laughed), Karl (fell)
2) It (is), I (like)
3) Ivy Jenkins (had finished), she (treated)
4) Everybody (knows), your husband (has treated)
5) Noise (can damage)

Exercise 29

1) The decision has been made by Mr Matthews.
2) Every lettuce has been flattened/was flattened by hailstones.
3) The Prime Minister has been interrupted repeatedly by hecklers.
4) All ticket holders will be reimbursed by the management.
5) The dolls' heads are made by Viola.
6) Flights were delayed for up to 72 hours by the French Air Traffic Controllers' strike.
7) This day will never be forgotten by me.
8) All the nuts had been eaten by the birds.
9) Every bedding plant and shrub will probably be uprooted by vandals.
10) Cruelty to animals is loathed by everyone here.

Exercise 30

1) Lord Kinross answered the telephone.
2) You/one should eat syllabub slowly with a tiny spoon.
3) He has spent all his pocket money.
4) Sullen grey clouds obscured the sun.
5) An intruder had forced the locks.
6) The people of Dominica will never forget this incident.
7) The suggestion outraged Mrs Sinclair.
8) She gave her answer in a low voice.
9) When will Mrs Phelps iron these shirts?
10) The union has called off the docks strike.

Exercise 31

1) a
2) a
3) b
4) b
5) a

Exercise 32

1) to apologise
3) to describe
4) to express
6) to explain
10) to observe

Exercise 33

Suggested answers:
1) As she stumbled . . .
2) When he examined . . .
3) As you drive . . .
4) When they had climbed . . .
5) As I am . . .
6) As we walked . . .
7) When he was sitting . . .
8) While he was imprisoned . . .
9) The whole family enjoys pork if it is roasted carefully
10) While he was travelling . . .

Exercise 34

1) my sitting
2) his joining
3) our complaining
4) my asking
5) our buying

Exercise 35

1) we
2) is, am standing, nod, bow, might say, scrape, happens, trembles
3) rooted
4) obscured
5) is obscured
6) to be (active), to be enrooted (passive)
7) verbal adjective (enterprising) or (engaging); forms tense (are being)
8) commemorating, inviting

Exercise 36

Suggested answers:

1) The incline was steeper than we thought.   (noun)
   I am inclined to agree with you.   (verb)
2) The fire is still raging.   (noun)
   Now it is your turn to fire questions.   (verb)
3) I have left all the refuse by the front gate.   (noun)
   I refuse to answer that question.   (verb)
4) You have won first prize.   (noun)
   My father prized honesty above all other virtues.   (verb)
5) Southsea is a popular seaside resort.   (noun)
   I hope I do not have to resort to bribery.   (verb)
6) For a short spell, she worked as a traffic warden.   (noun)
   Can you spell DISAPPOINTED?   (noun)
7) You'll need a permit to enter the enclosure.   (noun)
   Nobody is permitted to enter.   (verb)
8) The entrance is on the left.   (noun)
   She entranced everybody with her charm.   (verb)
9) The child had a violent temper.   (noun)
   The craftsman tempered the steel expertly.   (verb)
10) The nest held a clutch of eggs.   (noun)
    Clutch the rail tightly.   (verb)
11) The grate was empty of coal.   (noun)
    Grate the cheese finely.   (verb)
12) I may send her a Christmas hamper.   (noun)
    She was hampered in the chase by her long skirt.   (verb)
13) You have a nasty cough.   (noun)
    Try not to cough so loudly.   (verb)
14) The project is worth 50 per cent of the marks.   (noun)
    Try to project your voice to the back of the hall.   (verb)
15) The stem of the pipe was broken.   (noun)
    The little Dutch boy tried to stem the flow of water through the hole in the dyke.   (verb)
16) The smell of incense is very beautiful.   (noun)
    I was incensed by his attitude.   (verb)

17) Your sense of smell is almost non-existent.   (noun)
He could sense my disbelief.   (verb)
18) Use whatever form you wish.   (noun)
Form a circle at the back of the stage.   (verb)
19) I'm sure that tree is a pine rather than a cypress.   (noun)
The dog pined for his master.   (verb)
20) He has kept that ferret for ten months.   (noun)
She ferreted through his belongings.   (verb)

Exercise 37
1) would reply
2) had crashed
3) could
4) would be
5) would come

Exercise 38
1) chosen		11) ate
2) bought		12) led
3) knew		13) saw
4) lost		14) given
5) passed		15) taught
6) loosened		16) lent
7) woven		17) hid
8) heard		18) did
9) shod		19) chose
10) brought		20) caught

Exercise 39
1) shall
2) will
3) will
4) shall, will
5) shall

Exercise 40
Suggested answers:
1) ... if I were seriously overweight.
2) ... to visit Holland at some point.
3) ... if he is earning over £50 a week.
4) ... if he could afford it.
5) ... but we'll ask someone more reliable.

Exercise 41
1) enjoy
2) is
3) have
4) is
5) has

Exercise 42
1) quickly
2) tentatively
3) sadly
4) perhaps
5) now
6) almost
7) rarely
8) away
9) best
10) faster

Exercise 44
1) more quickly
2) better
3) wrongly
4) worse
5) earlier
6) more neatly than
7) more slowly
8) carefully
9) gracefully
10) well

Exercise 45
1) owing to
2) owing to
3) owing to
4) due to
5) due to

Exercise 46

1) a) Children enjoy ice-cream in the summer but nobody else does.
   b) Children enjoy ice-cream in the summer but they don't enjoy eating anything else.
   c) Children enjoy ice-cream in the summer but at no other time.

2) a) You can buy nothing but fish and chips here on Wednesdays.
   b) Fish and chips are sold here on Wednesdays but nothing else is done to them (i.e. cooking!)
   c) You can buy fish and chips here on one day a week, Wednesdays.
   d) You can buy fish and chips at no other place but here on Wednesdays.

3) a) Coffee and nothing else is served at 10.00 a.m.
   b) Coffee will be served at 10.00 a.m. and at no other time.
   c) Coffee will be served at 10.00 a.m. but nothing else will be done with it or done to it.

Exercise 47

1) but
2) or
3) but
4) and
5) or
6) and
7) but
8) or
9) and
10) and

Exercise 49

1) although
2) if
3) as
4) that
5) whenever
6) as if
7) so that
8) unless
9) since
10) before

Exercise 50

Suggested answers:

1) If you want to fight decay, clean . . .
2) I know you took the money because . . .
3) Although Shaun is very immature, I can't help . . .
4) After you left the house, Marva . . .
5) After Anna had accepted the post, she began to have doubts as . . .
6) If you are no better in the morning, call . . .
7) I asked her thirty years ago to be my wife and . . .
8) I cannot come because I . . .
9) Although you are small, you . . .
10) If your brother enjoys orienteering, he . . .

Exercise 51

First extract	Second extract
whether	as
or	and
where	and
and	if
if	and
when	if
if	and
as	and
	and

Exercise 52

1) Clare is not only a good swimmer but also an excellent flautist.
2) Marcel is interested not only in vintage cars but also in old agricultural machinery.
3) The girls beat the boys not only at hockey but also at basket ball.
4) He not only stole the money but he also told me a lie.
5) She was not only hurt but also bewildered.

Exercise 53

1) or
2) nor
3) nor
4) or
5) nor

Exercise 54

1) to
2) to
3) with
4) on
5) of
6) in
7) with
8) from
9) of
10) to

Exercise 55

1) ... was angered by and disgusted with ...
2) Where is my pencil?
3) To whom are you writing that letter?
4) ... persisted in ...
5) Compare this diamond with ...
6) The faulty goods were returned to the firm.
7) The apparatus comprised a bunsen burner, ...
8) ... was shared among ...
9) ... is something I am not prepared to put up with.
10) ... when I jumped off the bus.

Exercise 56

1) dissuade from
2) gloat over
3) aspire to
4) encroach on
5) comply with
6) centre on
7) advance towards
8) protest at
9) consist of
10) revolve around

Exercise 57

1) sympathetic to
2) indifferent to
3) deficient in
4) similar to
5) capable of
6) different from
7) oblivious to
8) responsible for
9) ignorant of
10) superior to

Exercise 58

1) as
2) like
3) like
4) as
5) as
6) like
7) as
8) like
9) as
10) as

Exercise 61

Suggested answers:

1) and
2) She is not only a part-time teacher but also a part-time physiotherapist.
3) or
4) Unless you put down a deposit for the flat now, you . . .
5) but

Exercise 62

I was deeply apprehensive at the prospect.
I didn't mind admitting it.
He wouldn't listen to me.
He was blind to my lack of basic survival skills.
He was utterly convinced of my eligibility to be a team member.
I was afraid of heights.
I could not swim.
I could not canoe.
I was on the verge of a nervous breakdown.
He swept every objection aside.

Exercise 63

1) I do appreciate your kindness.
2) In conclusion, I must issue a general warning.
3) I must know your destination.
4) The child's distress was clear to everyone.
5) The committee listened gravely to the Sanitary Engineer's recommendations.

Exercise 65

Suggested answers:

1) I cannot laugh because ...
2) Although it's very small, it's pretty.
3) If you want to raise money, do ...
4) Before Helen Derwent bought her return ticket, she ...
5) After the mysterious stranger finished his soup, he ...

Exercise 67

1) godmother
2) examination
3) anyone
4) author
5) earrings
6) man (and man refers to Hardy)
7) meal
8) people (and people refers to the Howitts)
9) sister
10) excuse

Exercise 69

1) Eleanor, whose cat was run over last weekend, is still very upset.
2) *Robinson Crusoe*, whose opening sentence immediately captures the reader's attention, is an eighteenth-century novel.
3) *Syndrome* is a noun whose meaning always eludes me.
4) It is a verdict whose effects will be far-reaching.
5) Our neighbours, whose house was burnt down yesterday, are on holiday in France and know nothing about it.
6) I'm looking for a bed whose overall length is more than six foot.
7) No one whose house has been haunted will fail to believe in ghosts.
8) This is the friend whose wife you met in Bangkok.
9) The mother whose child won the fancy-dress competition is a professional dressmaker.
10) Peter, whose peace of mind is enviable, has few possessions.

Exercise 71

1) intentions
2) cancellation
3) proposal(s)
4) position/address
5) reaction
6) behaviour
7) dismissal
8) delay
9) plans
10) elopement

Exercise 72
Suggested answer:

1) Until her marriage in 1854 to the Revd A. Nicholls, Charlotte Bronte (1816–55) lived in Haworth Parsonage, overlooking the cemetery and surrounded by the Yorkshire Moors. Her mother having died when Charlotte was a child, her family consisted of the following members: the Revd Patrick Bronte; younger sisters Anne and Emily (also novelists); Branwell Bronte, a talented artist but a heavy drinker. Although her first novel *The Professor* was not published until after her death, the other three novels were published in her lifetime within five years of each other: *Jane Eyre* (1847), *Shirley* (1849), *Villette* (1852).

Exercise 73
Suggested answer:

A very good recipe for flapjacks

Melt 300 g butter or margarine gently in a saucepan before stirring in thoroughly 150 g golden syrup, 150 g demerera sugar, 400 g quick porridge oats and a pinch of salt. Turn the mixture into a very large greased Swiss roll tin (approximately 40 × 30 cm), spread smoothly, and bake in the middle of a moderate oven (Gas Mark 4, 375°F) for about half an hour. Allow to cool before cutting into 60 fingers.

Exercise 74
Suggested answer:

Mrs Pront, grumbling that it was a bitterly cold Easter, told Mrs Green that they had planned to take the caravan to North Devon but had changed their minds as it was too cold for the outdoor life. Mrs Green readily agreed, declaring that it was the worst Easter that she had ever known. However, since she was expecting her daughter and seven grandchildren to arrive the next day, she thought she probably wouldn't notice the weather at all as she would have her hands so full.

Exercise 75
Suggested answer:

Mrs Baines asked her daughter what she had for homework that night. Sharon moaned that she had four subjects and that all the work had to be handed in the next day. Mrs Baines felt sorry for her daughter but she concealed this and approached the problem more practically by suggesting that Sharon got half the work out of the way by dealing with two subjects before supper. The thirteen-year-old snorted her derision, unimpressed by this solution.

Exercise 81

1) Scattered litters
2) Hibachi-style charcoal barbecues
3) Applying the plaster

Exercise 82

1) First sentence
2) Second sentence
3) Sally heard the word food, saw where Sandya was pointing and was off . . .
4) First sentence
5) Second sentence

Exercise 83

3 2 4 1 5   or   3 5 1 2 4